An Inner Strength

Quakers and Leadership

Edited by Kathy Hyzy

Published by Friends Bulletin Corporation
United States of America
Friends Bulletin Corporation is the publisher of *Western Friend*, the
official publication of Pacific, North Pacific, and Intermountain Yearly
Meetings of the Religious Society of Friends.
Opinions expressed in this book are of the authors, not necessarily of
the Yearly Meetings.

Cover design by Meredith Jacobson
Sight&Sense, www.sightandsense.com

Table of Contents

Introduction

The Nobel Committee awarded the Nobel Peace Prize to a religious organization for the first time in 1947. That organization was the Quakers, with the award accepted by the American Friends Service Committee and their British counterparts, the Friends Service Council. The Nobel Committee called out the Friends for hundreds of years of commitment to peace work, and for their utter dedication to relief efforts for victims of the two world wars.

In the award speech, Gunnar Jahn, chairman of the Nobel Committee, said, "The Society of Friends has never had many members, scarcely more than 200,000 in the entire world, the majority living in the United States and in England. But it is not the number that matters. What counts more is their inner strength and their deeds."

Since the inception of the Religious Society of Friends in the 1600's, the influence of Quakers has been felt far more widely and deeply than their numbers ought to allow. What *is* it about the faith and practices of Friends that allows them such influence? How does the commitment to peace, community engagement, simple living, and following the Inner Guide turn out leaders like Henry Cadbury and the hundreds of nameless Friends whose service to the victims of war so inspired the Nobel Committee?

Sixty-odd years have passed since Gunnar Jahn spoke those words, and in many ways, the Religious Society of Friends has faded from the consciousness of Americans. Still we have continued; Quakers had children who grew up to become Quakers themselves (known as "birthright" Friends), and individual Friends were quietly instrumental in the Civil Rights movement in the 1960's and 70's, where their example inspired others to join the faith. During the Korean and Vietnam Wars, when the draft attempted to conscript men opposed to the war, some found Quakers who walked them through the ordeal of trying to establish conscientious objector status. Many of these individuals went on to join Quaker congregations (often called meetings), as they became 'convinced' of the rightness of this community's calling as peacemakers in the world.

To Friends everywhere who are so concerned about how many Quakers there are (or aren't) in the United States today: I remind you that conversion and salvation have never been the point of our faith. George Fox's revelation back in 1652 was that he could have a direct and personal relationship with Christ, or God, or Spirit—terms we are more likely to use today. And in that direct relationship, he discovered both great joy and tremendous challenges. It often is not easy to listen to the promptings of the Spirit, and harder still to do what those promptings require. Being faithful to those promptings, to the best of our ability, is the point. It is our example that draws in new Friends, and keeps longtime Friends coming back.

And to those who are new to Quakers: The Friends who have contributed to this anthology are part of a long tradition. We seek to foster a direct and personal relationship with God. Because we believe each person has this capacity, some branches of Quaker tradition (though not all) do not have appointed pastors, for any one of us can listen for the promptings of the Spirit, and speak them aloud. But Friends are and always have been scattered far and wide, and so we have relied upon personal letters of testimony to share our experiences of God. We sometimes use words in ways you may find unusual; it's my hope that we have explained ourselves well enough for you to get the meaning behind the words. If not, ask a Quaker!

About This Book

I invite you to think of this book as a written Meeting for Worship. If you have never attended an 'unprogrammed' (meaning there is no pastor or planned service) Quaker meeting, that will be difficult, so I'll give you a quick description. It's an hour spent in a quiet room, where everyone—Quaker or not—is invited. Those who attend sink into the stillness and seek a connection with the Divine. Some call this 'waiting worship.' Sometimes it is silent for the hour. More often, several people feel moved by the Spirit to share a message. They stand, speak, and sit down. No response is given, though sometimes one person's words will build upon another's. And that is the sermon.

There are *so* many Quakers who could contribute to this book. I am inspired just thinking of those leaders who are absent from it! Like a Meeting for Worship, we have here the gifts of those who were willing and able to show up. Friends of color, Friends under forty, Friends over eighty, and those from pastoral traditions of Quakerism are all under-represented, if they are here at all.

An Inner Strength does represent one population reasonably well: eighteen of the twenty-two authors either currently hail from a Western state or spent some number of years here. This is partly by design; Western Friend endeavors to first and foremost serve and celebrate unprogrammed Friends in the Western US. It also reflects the fact that though far fewer Quakers live in this part of the country, we are disproportionately in leadership positions at Quaker organizations. It turns out it is easier to get a Quaker to admit they are a leader if they have served one of these organizations, though some of the best Quaker leaders are found elsewhere. I think this in part reflects our own ambivalence with leadership, something Robin Mohr speaks to in the prologue when she asks, "Is it *wrong* to have ambition to be faithful on a large scale?" Doug Bennett addresses it more explicitly in the final essay of this book.

While this book contains inspirational stories and thoughtful reflections from Quakers with insight into the nature of leadership among Friends, it's not a how-to manual for those seeking a more egalitarian model of leadership. Experience is the best teacher, and perhaps these stories will inspire in you a willingness to seek out opportunities to lead differently, from a deeper place—or to offer your support to those in leadership positions. For each section I have written a brief introduction and a few queries to help frame your reading, especially if you are using this book for study. You will notice the same themes over and over—the virtues of humility, obedience and patience surface time and again.

I am thankful to the Clarence and Lilly Picket Endowment for Quaker Leadership for underwriting some of the cost of creating this book—and for their ongoing dedication to fostering the creative development of Quaker leaders today. I am also grateful to the many Friends who cheered me on and provided thoughtful feedback. Special thanks go to Margery Post Abbott and Leni Skarin for their help. Thanks, too, to each of you who took the time to write down your witness to be shared in this collection. We all are enriched by your work.

With Gratitude,

Kathy Hyzy, Editor

Prologue

WHO'S GONNA FILL THEIR SHOES?

Robin Mohr

> *Who's gonna fill their shoes?*
> *Who's gonna stand up tall?*
> *Who's gonna play the Opry and the Wabash Cannonball?*
> *Who's gonna give their heart and soul to get to me and you?*
> *Lord, I wonder, who's gonna fill their shoes?*
>
> *-George Jones*

RUFUS JONES (1863-1948) is one of my heroes. He did so many things in his lifetime. He helped Friends and others to reconcile modern science and religious faith, to remember that Christian faith requires us to be active in the world, not just pious in a sterile meetinghouse, and he worked for peace and reconciliation within the Religious Society of Friends and in the wider world. That story you've heard about the Quakers who went to Germany to try to convince the Gestapo to let the Jews go? Yeah, Rufus Jones was one of them. And he was a great storyteller.

He also authored a rewrite of Quaker history to show an unjustifiable connection to the mystical tradition in Europe. He spoke every. single. time. and at great length in meeting for worship at Haverford College, for which he was mocked by students. In the last week, I've heard people criticize both his emphasis on mysticism without conversion of life and his emphasis on works over the transcendent. And I've heard he was a terrible driver. A man of giant gifts, giant vision and giant mistakes. That's okay, he is still one of my heroes. I think it's a form of idolatry to expect that our heroes must be perfect in every way. But who could possibly fill his shoes?

When I wrote a blog post in 2010 about all the imminent turnover in Quaker organizations, I wondered, "Will all these institutions survive this once in a lifetime mass shift in leadership? How many will move in new and vibrant directions? Are there too many openings at one time? Are there enough younger Friends who are ready, willing and able to take on new responsibilities? To take on the hard work and hard choices? To commit?" And then I responded, "I continue to reflect on these questions and where I might feel called to serve. I think that some of us need to step up to the plate." As I look around almost three years later, of the twenty or so organizations I can think of that have changed leaders, all of them found adequate applicants. About a quarter of them chose people younger than fifty, and almost half chose women. I've met most of these people and I have confidence that they are willing to take on hard work and move in new and vibrant directions. But I can tell you that none of them feels adequate to fill Rufus Jones's shoes.

Rufus Jones wrote something like 57 books and gave thousands of speeches all over the world. I can barely write a blog post once a month. But before I get too caught up in comparing myself to him, I have to remind myself that he had a wife, and a housekeeper, and a driver, and probably a series of typists to help him out. He wasn't cleaning his own bathroom. He probably never changed a diaper. Times have changed, and there are limits to how much he can serve as a role model for me.

Still, this brings me to considering how I am stepping up to the plate in my world.

Sheryl Sandberg's new book *Lean In* has been on my mind. If you haven't heard one of Sheryl Sandberg's talks or read her book, you can go to her new website, www.LeanIn.org. Now the COO of Facebook, she is encouraging women to take professional risks, to push for a seat at the table at work and for equality at home, to not give up on their careers just because it's so damn hard when your kids are little. It's controversial, as important conversations are. For me, it helps to articulate that I have leaned in hard this last couple of years. And I have been supported at home and in my meetings, and by many Friends. But is it enough? Am I doing enough? Or doing it well enough?

I like to think that I am not aiming to be as famous or influential as Rufus Jones, but I am working on being as faithful to the calling I have, to live up to the Light that I have been given. Leaning in hard can still look undramatic and unheroic. I suspect that Rufus Jones did aim to be dramatic and heroic and that's one of the things that annoyed people. How is that different from singers giving their heart and soul to get to me and you?

Is it *wrong* to have ambition to be faithful on a large scale?

At meeting on Sunday, I asked God that question. One of the things I forever appreciate about unprogrammed Quaker meetings is the opportunity to bring my inarticulate mess to God in prayer. I don't have it all figured out, and that's okay. I can just hold my swirling questions in the Light. And sometimes there's an answer. Not a booming voice from beyond the ceiling, but a quiet knowing of something new.

God's answer was like this: "So what are you doing for those who will come after you?"

Huh? I'm the one who is looking for role models, and instead I'm being asked to *be* one. Not by any actual younger people, mind you, just by God. Darn. Now what?

Recently I found a 35-year-old report that could have been written last month on leadership in the Religious Society of Friends. It turns out that the same issues have been troubling us for at least that long. Lack of trust, lack of shared vision, need for divine guidance and human accountability, unclear relationships between individuals, monthly meetings/churches and larger institutions.

Some of the solutions the report suggested would still be functional. One of the problems with not having enough leadership is that good solutions don't get implemented.

Rufus Jones, for all his foibles, was strongly committed to encouraging and supporting younger generations, and they loved him for it. Two of my very favorite Rufus Jones speeches were both given to Young Adult Friends, at their invitation, when he was about eighty years old. Perhaps I can aspire to be like him in this regard and let go of the temptation to try to be like him in other ways.

I can still give my heart and soul for the Religious Society of Friends. Thy will, Lord, not mine.

Both these favorite speeches of mine are available online: "The Vital Cell," William Penn Lecture, 1941, http://pamphlets.quaker.org/wpl1941a.html and "What Will Get Us Ready?", Baltimore Young Friends Yearly Meeting Lecture, 1944, http://www. friendsjournal.org/what-will-get-us-ready/.

Listening

Margery Post Abbott
Nadine Hoover
Ashley M. Wilcox
Christine Betz Hall

L ISTENING IS AT THE HEART of faith for Quakers. In 1652, when George Fox had the experiences that led to the creation of the Religious Society of Friends, it was listening that set him on fire. In the England of his time, only priests were understood to have the ability to hear God, and typically, God's voice was found in the texts of the Bible. Fox was a deeply spiritual young man, dissatisfied with the ways of the church (as were many at the time), and he spent years wandering, seeking and praying. Finally, one day God spoke to him.

In our modern world of plurality and debate about the nature (or existence of God), it's difficult to understand what a revelation this must have been. But it was, and it was utterly transformative for Fox, and for those who heard his message and joined with him. It was so transformative that these Quakers- as they came to be known for the quaking they often exhibited during worship- were willing to risk imprisonment, persecution and death for fealty to one simple Truth: that God (for them, Christ) continued to be present and accessible, and that anyone could hear the voice of God.

Granted, it was not easy. Anyone who has read any part of the Bible understands that a relationship with the Christian God is not straightforward. The experience of Friends then and now has been that God speaks in a "still, small voice." And so Friends developed an unusual style of church: instead of a pastor preaching from a pulpit and the usual trappings of a Sunday morning service, they gathered together to "wait on the Lord." They sat in chairs in homes at first, then concentric circles or arcs of pews in what came to be known as meetinghouses. And they sat and waited, in silence, until someone felt the motion of the Spirit, and stood and spoke whatever message the Lord had asked them to speak. Sometimes an hour of expectant, listening silence would pass unbroken. More often, in these early time of Quakerism, the messages came frequently, from men and women both, and at some length; it is said that George Fox once spoke for three hours straight! Most importantly, they understood

2

that listening for the voice of God was an individual activity practiced in community. What was heard was shared, and in the sharing, the authenticity of the message was tested.

The entire orientation of early Friends was devoted to improving their spiritual hearing, so to speak; in addition to waiting worship, they developed a tradition of plain, simple clothing and furnishings, so as to avoid distraction from the message of God. They read and studied the Bible, preparing their minds and hearts for the messages they might receive. And they wrote voluminously and eloquently of their experiences of God, of their struggles to follow the Truths the Spirit spoke to them, and of those moments of profound connection. The letters and journals of early Friends at times read like spiritual field guides, describing in great detail how it felt to directly experience the presence of God, to be moved to speak during waiting worship. These texts served, and continue to serve, as remarkable guideposts for others seeking to cultivate a similar relationship with the Spirit.

Today the Religious Society of Friends, particularly in America, has a more complicated family tree, with many different forms of worship taking place on Sundays. "Unprogrammed" Friends continue to practice waiting worship more or less as it first began, but even among Quakers who have pastors and Sunday services that would look familiar to your average churchgoer, the fundamental devotion to listening for that of God remains. And it is that devotion which is key to both developing strong leadership skills among Friends and to maintaining effective leadership within the tradition.

For Friends, listening has both an individual and corporate dimension, and the essays in this section speak to both. We begin with Margery Abbott, who shares the story of her surprising transformation from a shy, introverted Friend who avoided leadership positions, to a well-seasoned clerk who is often asked to serve on or lead committees. For her, leadership came from listening to the Inner Voice, and is not a mantle she would have taken up without its promptings and the gentle, direct support of other Quakers.

Nadine Hoover's inspirational story of her own experiences of experimenting with the Spirit reveals how deep one's relationship to that still, small voice can become. She and Margery both speak to the value of testing messages received from the Spirit with a community of grounded, trusted Friends who can help affirm the truths and weed out the places where one's own ego is getting in the way.

Ashley Wilcox and Christine Betz-Hall both share in greater detail the value of relying on others. Quakers have a long tradition of "eldering". This practice has in the past been abused by those who wished to exert control over others. But Friends today are rediscovering the value of having an experienced Friend or small group of Friends to rely on as "spiritual midwives" who offer guidance and support to Friends who are following the direction of some Truth they have been given.

Queries on Listening

Margery writes, "Answering that of God in the other is not possible if we can't recognize what is of God, and can't hear it in someone else's words and being." How do you see the writers in this section practicing active listening for "that of God"? And how do you feel it affects their ability to serve as leaders?

In your life and in your relationships, how do you work to overcome the tendency toward individualism?

If you were asked to be in a position of leadership, how would you work to take care of yourself? Whom might you ask to help you stay grounded, and why?

How does it feel to you to listen for the voice of the Spirit? How does it feel to you to listen deeply to another person? And how does it feel when someone else listens deeply to you?

LISTENING FOR THE VOICE OF THE LIGHT

by Margery Post Abbott

L EADERSHIP COMES in ways you may not be looking for. You walk into a new meeting, thinking you will quietly settle into the corner for worship on Sunday morning, and all too soon find yourself as clerk of a committee. That was my experience when I first began to attend Multnomah Meeting back in the late 1970s. While I had been a Friend all my life and attended meeting on and off through my twenties, I had managed to never serve on a committee until I moved to Portland. There, I was asked to clerk the first committee I was on. It was a good thing for me, and presumably for the community, as they kept asking me to do more.

Stepping into a leadership position may be natural, as when a few years later, it was obvious when I was to be clerk of the monthly meeting. It was late in the midst of the 10-plus-year seasoning process the meeting had been undergoing over whether we might marry gays and lesbians. It happened that Carl and I were 3,000 miles away during the spring when tensions rose to a point where many people behaved in hurtful ways. I was not surprised at all when I was approached to be clerk – I hadn't been there, had not angered anyone, and hadn't witnessed inappropriate behavior. I was the obvious person to step into the position at this time.

These initial experiences of taking leadership fit into my experience of secular action. I could use the very practical skills I had developed in my workplace and in such things as forming and chairing a National Organization for Women (NOW) chapter. I approached my work in the meeting in much the same manner, analyzing what needed to be done and figuring out the best way to proceed with the help of others on that committee or in the wider community. I was good at consensus building.

Then, unexpectedly, in the process of being clerk of the meeting in a tense and difficult situation, I had to dig deeper. The external skills took me only so far. I quickly realized I needed serious help. My natural instinct was to turn to books. I began reading everything I could get my hands on about Meeting for Worship for Business. I was grateful for the Worship and Ministry Committee meetings each month, the time we spent sharing with each other and the brainstorming we did over how to help the meeting. But all too often I was rushing into these meetings late, carrying the sandwich I had grabbed for supper as my work obligations meant long and sometimes intense days. Being staff for a group weighing the environmental effects of a proposed garbage incinerator provided me with both a valuable context and schooling in emotional responses: what was going on in meeting wasn't about Quakers per se, it was about the wider human condition. Our challenge as Friends was to find the strength to respond differently and not be caught in perpetual anger or identified by adversarial roles.

Two other dynamics were essential to my ability to grow into being a monthly meeting clerk: the lessons I began to learn from previous generations of Friends and the ongoing lessons in ways of listening. Both showed me the only true source of leadership was in the voice of the Inward Guide. When we act out of personal willpower, we can do a lot. But we can also sink into a morass of fear or arrogance, or be pulled unaware into the desire for success or the need for individual recognition, to the detriment of the community.

Spiritual Ancestors

It is rather intimidating to face a meeting full of strongly opinionated, angry, and/or deeply hurt individuals with the intent to conduct business. Those determined that Multnomah Meeting recognize same-sex marriage wanted it to happen now, and had run short of patience long ago. Those who still could not accept it were feeling more and more isolated. As was my habit, I turned to books and other writings for help. I found more than expected in some old family letters dating from the 19th century. I brought excerpts of these letters to business meeting, sharing vivid descriptions of Friends locking each other out of meetinghouses during the painful separations of 1827-28. My great-great-great grandfather wrote about his frustrations with the people in his meeting who were held up as wise, but who were intolerant of his anti-slavery activism as being too worldly. Such glimpses into our common past brought laughter and helped ease the anxiety and pressure to act too quickly.

Over the years, these and many other spiritual ancestors have reassured me during times of intense transformation and gave me language for strong spiritual openings. They offered me guidance in discerning the workings of the Light and how to separate that out from other voices in my head. They gave me courage as they told of their own fears and their own confidence in divine leadings. And they taught me to trust that Guide even when it made no sense to my intellectual self.

Paying Attention

Having always been a very quiet person, listening seemed like a natural part of my life. As long as I can recall, I preferred hearing what others had to say much more than sharing my thoughts. More than anything, I did not believe that I could have anything worth saying and I was unwilling to test this conviction. It took me years to understand that this was a passive listening, a stance controlled by fear.

This kind of passive listening included another negative dimension, in that I could carry on a commentary in my head about what the other person's meaning or motives were. Because I never spoke about what I was hearing, I had no way to discover whether my assumptions were valid. And, by not speaking my own reflections, I never had to make myself vulnerable, never had to reveal when I got things wrong.

And so I had to learn that listening also has an active, participatory dimension. I began to learn it when I started to let the other person know what I was hearing and finding out if it matched what they hoped to say. This sort of active attention is important for more verbal people to develop, too. For them, passive listening can occur when they break in and talk over the person attempting to speak. In this case the overly talkative listener doesn't worry whether what he or she says has anything to do with what was meant. In either case, talking may be happening and the ears may register sound waves, but no connection happens. There is no dialogue. There is nothing that might resemble the Quaker practice of "answering that of God in the other."

Multnomah Meeting offered a number of workshops in the 1980s that had to do with Quaker decision-making and focused on how we might listen to one another. I still have the sheets on how to listen better, which offer suggestions such as not preparing what one is going to say while the other person is speaking, reflecting back on what you have heard, and so on. These are great skills, some of which come out of mediation training, and are very useful in all kinds of situations. But they are only part of what Friends mean by listening.

Answering that of God in the other is not possible if we can't recognize what is of God or hear it in someone else's words and being. I first became aware of consciously listening for the Spirit while I was clerk of the meeting. Twice a month I had to close worship. Outwardly this was a very simple practice of shaking hands with the person next to me at eleven o'clock. I decided I would do this without wearing a watch. I would take seriously the possibility that it would be clear when it was time to close. I noticed the outward rhythms of people arriving, when the children came, when vocal ministry was offered. Then I became more aware of the meeting's condition: were many people restless? Was there a stillness in the room? I started to listen for whether someone was about to speak: was there something still to be said? Gradually I became more aware of the connections among us.

Several years later, a whole new dimension opened to me. The wall separating my outer and inner life cracked from the lightness of complete Love. A clear call was present with no words necessary even as people around me voiced messages which spoke to my condition. This mystical experience coalesced into a call to public ministry of writing and speaking about the work of the Eternal in my life and in the community of Friends.

The entire feel of taking up this work was unlike anything I had done in the past. The motion was fully within me, yet totally other. I felt supported and guided by all that gives life and breath. I was humbled by the work I needed to do to prepare myself to be able to respond to the call. Yet that work too was given by that Inward Guide, as was the directive to speak of this to others and gather a growing community into this work.

Listening to this guidance, which was beyond all words, set me forth on the ministry of articulating my faith, first in the written word and then gradually in the spoken word. It is hard to imagine a better example of God as Trickster: taking a most unlikely, inarticulate person and using her to voice one vision of who we are as Friends.

Recognizing the Inward Guide

When to engage. When to be patient. When to say "I did wrong." When to delight in knowing one is part of something wonderful. The possibilities are infinite. For those of us who love to think through every possibility, it is so tempting to stay with the tried and true, the familiar, the acceptable, the expected. Or, the bold among us may feel that their knowledge and reasoning will protect them and give a firm basis for radical, unexpected action. For either kind of person, the emotions may throw all reason in a heap. In old Quaker language, we might describe this in terms of lagging behind or running ahead of the Guide. Both result from not listening to the Voice of the Light that uses our intellectual capabilities and all our skills, even those we are not aware of. What is distinctive about this Holy Light is that it makes clear where reason becomes rationalizing, where confidence becomes arrogance, where care becomes dominated by fear.

Leadership as understood by Friends is a consequence of listening, attending, and cooperating with the transformative power of the Light. For some, this sounds feasible and natural. But living up to this can also be painful or frightening. Preparing to give talks or working on my writing, I often find that I have to pay attention to that fear and move towards it – it is an indicator of what I am to do. It is not unusual for this to lead to angry bargaining with God and other resistance. Faithfulness, in my experience, requires change in the depths of the soul again and again. This change paradoxically affirms the central uniqueness of one's being even as it turns everything sole-side-up.

When we are embedded in a community that can call us back to the central task presented to us by the Spirit, we are given an essential gift that includes support and accountability, both key to leadership. The most straightforward example of this for me was the time I received a phone call asking me to be clerk of Friends Committee on National Legislation (FCNL). This possibility had never hit my radar screen. I hadn't even been clerk of an FCNL committee. My impulse was to say "no," then hang up. Because I had an Anchor Committee,

I realized I had to at least tell them about this. They listened to all my reasons, asked many good questions, and were obviously relieved when I reluctantly heard what they had: this task was mine to take up.

So often over the years it has been the people around me who have seen the way forward for me. Some have named the books I was to work on, others invited me to step out into public roles, while others have affirmed me when the Spirit opened up new, unexpected directions.

A Vision Writ So That a Runner May Read It

Even as I was writing this essay, someone offered what I needed, as a friend sent an email referring me to chapter 2 of Habakkuk. The words of this minor prophet seem right for me in this time:

> I will stand at my watchpost,
> And station myself on the rampart;
> I will keep watch to see what he will say to me,
> And what he will answer concerning my complaint.
> Then the Lord answered me, and said:
> Write the vision;
> Make it plain on tablets,
> So that a runner may read it.
> For there is still a vision for the appointed time;
> it speaks of the end, and does not lie.
> If it seems to tarry, wait for it;
> it will surely come, it will not delay.

Habakkuk 2:1-3 (NRSV)

This admonition to stay on the ramparts and keep watch is quite timely, as everyone around me knows. I have been complaining constantly about my lack of clarity on what I am to write next. "Write the vision." What an instruction! I don't know yet what it means, but it has been handed to me as I write about the leadership that has been given to me to exercise, most centrally through the written word.

Reading on in Habakkuk, the prophet is given a strong, distasteful message that the Chaldeans will punish the Hebrews for having fallen away from God. Habakkuk is outraged that such evil folk are given this task, as they are prone to worse behavior than the Hebrews. He demands to know why the evil are not punished and why God is using the more evil to punish the less wicked. God responds that the

Chaldeans will also be punished, as will all those who are arrogant, greedy, plundering, shedding blood, doing violence and worshipping false Gods. Like Job, Habakkuk ends with a place of worship and rejoicing in faith even "though the fig tree does not blossom and no fruit is on the vines . . ."

I hear echoes of my spiritual ancestors in this as they focused on faithfulness rather than success. They also recognized that punishment was in divine hands, not human ones. The examples abound of traveling ministers who spoke, sometimes condemning, sometimes raising up, yet always moving on as they were led. It was not the minister's work to implement the message he or she carried, but that of the faithful community. What a counter-intuitive approach in this day and age of efficiency and individual responsibility! Sorting out what is mine to do is a challenge for each one of us, as is the recognition that each one of us is being called in some way into service and into living out God's way.

Walking with the Guide

When I am asked about my experience in leadership among Friends, two words often come to mind: humility and vulnerability, both tempered by community. At least, that is the story I have told, making it clear that struggles and doubts are present even when the touch of an all-embracing Love has cast out all doubt. In some ways my story is a very familiar one. The story is about someone who has been put into circumstances which press her greatest weaknesses into a tool which opens doors for others.

For me, listening for the Voice of the Infinite is at the core of humility. Listening for the divine spark in another person is of the essence in this call to be neither more nor less than those around us. The root meaning of humility is the same as that of *humus*, of the earth. It is about being grounded in that which is eternal, seeing that I am loved, and recognizing that the same is true for all others. Each person holds the potential to nourish and respond to the Seed of God within. When that happens, we each have the capacity to do amazing things and act without fear.

What may seem like risk-taking and courage from the outside can feel like reaching out with your last breath and grabbing a life preserver— or a response to a yearning so deep that not to act would be like choosing to starve. I love the 46th Psalm, and it seems to fit here to remember: "God is in the midst of the city; it shall not be moved; God will help it when the morning dawns, The nations are in an uproar, the kingdoms totter; he utters his voice, the earth melts."

The help we receive may be nothing like what we specifically hoped for or expected, but it will be evident. Sometimes what is called leadership simply means holding on to the calling, to the knowledge that Grace is present, even when everything seems to fall apart around you.

AN EXPERIMENT WITH SPIRIT

Nadine Hoover

M Y PERSONAL EXPERIENCE of a palpable, unified Spirit which
creates and animates all life is one reason I am a Friend. The
other is that I choose to experiment with this Spirit in shaping and
guiding my daily life. This is a consistent practice, which makes me
and other Friends reliable witnesses to the inward nature of things.
It puts our lives in an order that reflects the beauty and dignity of
life and makes us available and prepared when called upon to act.
Because this practice is traditional among Friends, I have seen others
turn to and trust us in times of great need or import. Leadership is an
outcome, not a concern, of this practice.

George Lakey defines Quaker leadership as "taking initiative in
relationships." Friends Peace Teams in Asia/West Pacific, which grew
out of my traveling ministry, focuses on building relationships, person
to person, but realizes that often the worst violence in the world is
perpetrated among loved ones, family, and neighbors. Friendship is
not enough. We build responsive relationships with people committed
to living peacefully and applying integrity in daily life, and we do this
work across a diversity of age, culture, religion, and background.

As Friends Peace Teams members visit with people who survived war
and natural disaster, many of our hosts are taken with the idea of
living by conscience, integrity and discernment. In this collaboration,

we have learned that this way of life requires social skills of affirming, listening, speaking, and cooperating; dialogue on the dynamics of violence, nonviolence and peace; a committment to being emotionally well; and a commitment to developing our capabilities to interact with others and natural materials. But most of all, we need to be convinced of the omnipresence and transforming power of life itself. It is present and exceeds all human tragedy, even when we are convicted (as in have clear convictions), fall short, are inadequate, or become the perpetrator or oppressor. Without this whole experience of the Living Spirit, any experiment with integrity in daily life tends toward egotistical self-absorption or rigid self-righteousness.

As Wilmer Cooper noted in his Pendle Hill pamphlet on the topic, practicing integrity is multifaceted. We manifest integrity through honesty or factuality; authenticity; and the matching of belief, word and action.

Relating to Truth

To be responsible is to be able to respond. The question is, to respond to what? The practice of Friends, once convinced and convicted, is to yield to the Spirit's universal nature and flow. None of us knows what inward nudging will be there when we listen, but when we do yield to the truth working within, the fruits of the Spirit arise: "love, joy, peace, long-suffering, gentleness, goodness, faith, meekness, temperance; against which there is no law." (Galatians 5:22-23) As these experiences grow in number, we come to trust that which rings of truth.

Contemporary Friends frequently jump to seeking "leadings", which one may imagine as seeking the place and activity in the world that is the most authentic for someone. When preoccupied by seeking leadings, however, the unwitting temptation is to avoid the truth working within, which is not typically packaged to our size.

In this work, I seldom receive truth that is "just my size." It's usually too small and inadequate. "If I were God it would not be like this," I rage. Or it's too huge and overwhelming. "I can't handle it!" I cry and turn away. But I have grieved, trembled and raged, physically discharging emotions that once overwhelmed me, leaving my attention free to be aware of and available to truth in all its sizes. Then I experiment with what is true in the endless elements of my daily life. This is what prepares me to be able to respond if called.

The heart of my personal experiment with Spirit lies in examining each element of my daily life and experimenting with shaping it to reflect my inward experience of the beauty, joy and dignity of life. Everything in my life extends from experiencing the Spirit that creates and animates the world. It is not a race to see when I can get it all right; it is a never-ending daily opportunity to engage, experiment and explore.

I consciously began this experiment in 1986. One of my early insights was that to be free to do what is right in every moment, I had to settle debts promptly—credit is for short-term cash-flow, not for long-term obligation. To me the implication of this was that I would never own a home since I could not imagine home ownership without a mortgage. Friends told me that was archaic thinking, a throwback from the agricultural era, not applicable in modern society. But this insight propelled me into a pay-as-you-go lifestyle where I have been free to respond to opportunities that have not been possible for debt-burdened Friends. Being debt free allowed me the liberty to act and take risks on a number of occasions: to speak out against corruption at work; leave high-paying jobs and face unemployment rather than collude with fear, self-interest and deception; sublet my house in order to travel in the ministry and eventually dedicate massive hours to expressing my conscientious objection to war and to forming Friends Peace Teams in Asia West Pacific.

Every day affords more moments to experiment with more aspects of life: the way I speak, use time, what I do, what I use, the way I organize relationships, and so forth. I regularly try to ask myself the question, "Does my current lifestyle help or hinder my awareness of the spirit?" This alone takes time and grows as I pay attention to it. Subsequent questions are: "How can I shape my outward life to express this inward experience—in my home, or at work, community, or play?" or "What truth is working in me and what are the implications for my life?"

Community for Feedback and Testing

As I practice being inwardly guided, the line between being inspired and neurotic becomes increasingly thin. An essential part of the practice is stopping, sharing stories of my decisions and actions, and responding to feedback. Early on, as I grew clearer and felt the power and liberty of conscience, I became impatient with others who dismissed my insights, held other priorities, or suggested I was excessive or just plain wrong. I remember feeling the community was not as dedicated or spiritually mature as I was becoming, yet as this thought crossed my mind I instantly could sense the convenience and attraction of narcissism. I realized we live in the web of society, and participation from all of us in that web is how peace is nurtured. So I slowed down, even stopped regularly, to allow the constraints of the community to temper my inspiration.

With both fellow conscientious objectors to war and spiritual companions for Friends Peace Teams in Asia/West Pacific, I share stories of the decisions I make and actions I take and listen to their direction and feedback. Others see what I cannot. Most people will not give honest feedback, however, unless I clearly and frequently voice a desire for feedback, then practice breathing and taking it in when it comes, especially when it comes in a form I'm not expecting. The longer I practice, the more I realize how important it is to remain open to feedback, no matter how certain I have become.

Giving honest feedback is emotionally complex. When giving feedback we need to be as affirming, specific, and concrete as possible. We are freer to give feedback if we trust that the person receiving it will not take offense, but will consider and weigh it for themselves, then in turn apply his or her own discernment concerning what rings true and what does not. For example, I weighed the feedback that settling debts promptly was arcane and no longer applied, but still the original insight did not leave me and I let this sense of what is true guide my decisions. Yet it was still immensely important to ask for and consider the feedback.

Basing the organization of Friends Peace Teams in Asia West Pacific on discernment, the coordinators have discovered the value of listening carefully to one another. Past distresses frequently impinge, whether things are going well or not. When the words don't feel like they are in the Spirit, whether we like or agree with what is being said or not, we have learned to stop and inquire.

•*Have you heard me?* In other words, it feels like you are thinking about your own idea, not listening, and so you are not actually hearing what is being said.

•*Are you taking this personally?* In other words, it feels like you are taking this personally when it is not at all about you.

•Is that frustration I hear? In other words, it feels like your disappointment in past similar situations is flooding our success right now, which is enormously confusing; just appreciate and say thank you for what is new.

•Is this extra effort? Extra effort beyond what is minimally necessary turns into damage, often to inflate our sense of self or accomplishment; let go of all extra effort.

Among early Friends, this experiment with spitirual guidance was referred to as "the rising of the Christ within." Convinced and convicted, they believed that they could convert their lives to be Christ, manifesting God within and through them. They established monthly meetings to test individual discernment, recognizing that such an audacious project needed the tending and tempering of the community. Friends testified to what they needed to have or to let go of in order to keep their awareness of the spiritual life alive, and how the spirit was shaping and guiding them. The community was asked not if they liked, agreed with or even understood, but whether or not it felt like it was coming from the Living Spirit. If so, the community recorded the testimony in the book of minutes. If the entire community recognized something was true for all of them, then it was recognized as a "corporate testimony."

If Friends collectively placed our faith in this experiment today, we would produce contemporary social testimonies out of the fabric of our interwoven lives, not out of strategic thinking. Again, Quaker testimonies do not necessarily produce spiritual life, but rather our faith in experimenting with the Spirit in our lives produces testimonies. Making this experimental practice primary in life and relying on community feedback, although rare today, is essential to the Religious Society of Friends and what makes us who we are.

Being Available and Prepared

Living with an awareness of the dignity and worth of all life frees me from having to do anything in order to earn value. I work to change myself before I go about to change others, simply for the sheer joy of it. I have friends and community who know me and have affirmed my path on every step. I know they will be there with me, although they cannot rescue me from my own life and the consequences of my actions. I'm busy, but available to drop what I am doing and attend to what is needed. I'm obligated to no debts or plans beyond doing my best to do what is right in any moment. No success or failure will change my measure of worth.

Over the years, the Spirit has made use of my availability in ways large and small. In 2006, an earthquake took out a communications trunk line outside of Taiwan, disrupting communications to Aceh precisely when the Tamiang River poured sixteen-foot floods and three to four feet of muck over vast areas of East Aceh, Tamiang, and North Sumatra. No news of our friends there was forthcoming. My friends in a hair salon in Alfred, New York said to me, "Just go." So I did. At another time, Indonesian authorities closed down a government office assigned to relocate several thousand people displaced by the war in Aceh, who were afraid that after the government stopped trying to relocate them that people with significant financial interests would come with bulldozers in the middle of the night to drive them out. Knowing that my presence would protect them, again friends in Alfred said, "Just go." So I did.

I went because I was available to go. My relationships, home, finances, and health were in order. But I am equally available in small ways, ways in which I notice people I pass in the street, talk to people I chance to meet, stop or change course any number of times during the day to attend to things as they present themselves.

Attending to the presence

Clearly the power of life and Spirit is present in every moment, whether or not I am working to notice it. Every breath is animated. I will not stop breathing if I stop noticing the source from which breath comes, but noticing it changes me and the way I perceive power. And as this power is present in every moment, it is present in the hard times as well as the good times. The moments that we are inadequate, overwhelmed, or wrong give us the opportunity to see beyond ourselves, to lift up our chins and see the great power and value of life. The more we are acquainted with this power in the hard and treacherous times as well as the good and glorious times, the richer our experience and language of it, the greater our awareness is of its immensity.

Trauma sets in when a person is overwhelmed and freezes, when needs appear to outstrip our ability to respond or adapt. People who are alert to the power of life may often be able to face the worst, as well as the best, of human existence without feeling overwhelmed, because the needs can never outstrip the immensity of this power. I have learned to release emotions through crying, sobbing, trembling, shouting, or laughing without shame or reluctance.

Herein lies the seat of humility; only in the midst of our shortcomings and inadequacies is the magnitude of our dignity and worth revealed. Without flaws, we would not encounter this creative force beyond our own ego, unconditionally granting us life. Herein lies religious conviction as well. To be fully aware of our enormous shortcomings opens our capacity to see beyond our own ego. Conviction is steadfast and does not waver with one's passing fancies, emotions, desires or rationales, but weathers personal idiosyncrasies, anchored in a knowledge and reality beyond one's self.

When I began to experiment with noticing the goodness and power of life within and around me, I wrote in my journal what percentage of the day I stayed aware of the Spirit. It wavered, rose, and fell. I thought 15% was good. I wondered if it could go up and felt strong when it rose more often to 20%. Then like passing through a threshold, it rose high, 60% to 70%. Within weeks it was hard not to see the living spirit in any person or thing!

Yet still, as I sat in the mornings for ten, twenty, thirty minutes or whatever was needed, the truth working within me was often not what I would want. When it came, I sometimes hesitated and felt an impulse to return to the silence saying, "Give me any guidance but that!" When I was struggling in a difficult relationship, what came to me one morning was a voice that said, "You're asking the wrong question. God does not care if you stay together or separate; God wants you to live rightly." Without missing a beat, I felt my own voice say, "And this is wrong." This was not at all what I wanted, but I knew it was true and I felt the peace. Another time I woke in the middle of the night to a voice, "Why did you sign that contract? Don't you know you're leaving?" It was the only time my life I sat straight up in bed, shocked. "What do you mean, I'm leaving? Am I leaving? Could I leave?" I realized my partners at work were basing decisions on distresses and personal comfort, not on what was right. I went in calm and clear to submit my resignation.

Being prepared is both inward and outward. The inward preparation is a full sense of worth and trust in the truth. The outward preparation is an increasingly well-tuned capacity to perceive what is true or not in all things big and small.

To Whom Others Turn

Friends who engage in this experiment with Spirit come to know things for what they are, rather than how they appear. Because of this, others turn to Friends in times of greatest need or import, when the truth and trust are needed. We become the witnesses whom the community calls upon to testify to what is right and just and what is not. People support and believe in us, but only when they see the change in us that comes about from the doing of this work and only if we hold close to the humility and availability it affords. Our work is recognized more by what we are and how we're available, our "not doing," shaped and defined by what we do when no one is looking. Our practice permeates and shapes our whole person.

Traveling with Friends Peace Teams in Asia West Pacific, I met the imam of a community of people displaced by the war in Aceh into the mountains of North Sumatra. They were a closed community before I arrived. He was anxious that I was getting close to people there. It took me awhile before I could understand what he was asking, then I said, "Oh, you want to know what I promised and to whom to get the resources to be here!" He said, "Exactly." I told him the only promise I made was that we would make the best decisions we could about what was right, and describe our decisions and actions to our respective communities.

I explained to him that my community of supporters wanted to hear stories of our work together. If we planted chili, they wanted to know how many, how far apart, how deep, what time of year and if there was a threat of flooding. If we built a school, they wanted to know how deep the foundation was, where the wood came from, how the roof was vented and how many square meters per child. But these supporters far away cannot use their money, power, or influence to demand what the imam's community would decide or do.

The imam was amazed, relieved, and clear; this was consistent with his experience of us, but different from any other experience he'd had. Other outsiders had always come with a predetermined agenda, independent of anyone local. They wanted stories to take back and sell for donations to support wages that far exceed what anyone local could imagine. I affirmed that we wanted to do the work together as an opportunity to get to know and learn from one another.

This imam was describing well-intentioned people who spend too much time living in strategies, plans, and constructions, not out interacting with people and materials vastly different than those to which they were acucstomed. Spirit, however, lives in those direct relationships between people and with nature.

The influence of members of the Religious Society of Friends has often reached far beyond our numbers. We've managed to do so much with so few, not because of some great skill in planning or need to do so, but because of our attention to personal change and doing what's right regardless of whether or not it seems petty or overwhelming, whether or not it will make a difference. As one Friend says, it's showing up, paying attention, telling the truth, and not being attached to the outcome.

When I had the opportunity to meet Vietnamese government officials, I asked why it was that Friends were allowed in Vietnam when the country was closed to all foreigners. They replied that Friends were the only people who took no side and treated everyone openly and equally; there were no secrets and no one was an enemy. Experimenting with the Spirit each day changes us, beyond words or wishfulness, in ways that others recognize, trust, and turn to.

TAKING CARE OF THE BABY:
SELF-CARE AND SUPPORT IN MINISTRY

Ashley M. Wilcox

I DO NOT have children of my own, but babies have provided powerful imagery for me in my ministry. In 2010, I served as co-clerk of the planning committee for the Pacific Northwest Quaker Women's Theology Conference. As co-clerk, I oversaw every aspect of planning the conference, from finding the location to choosing a theme and asking volunteers to give plenary talks, facilitate small groups, and lead worship. The rest of the planning committee and I had spent two years brainstorming, meeting, and organizing, but the month before the conference was the busiest time. I had left my full-time job and was released for ministry for the summer, so I took responsibility for a lot of the last-minute details. I was constantly worried that I was forgetting something important.

A few days before the conference began, I had a vivid dream. In the dream, I was at the women's conference, talking with a friend. My friend turned to me and said, "You know what you forgot, right?" I panicked and said, "No, what did I forget?" She responded, "You forgot about the baby!" I looked over and saw the baby. It was sickly, naked, and cold, crying alone in a crib. I woke up distressed that I had forgotten about the baby.

A friend who knows more about interpreting dreams than I do once told me that everyone in the dream is me. As I thought about the dream, I knew that I was me, and that my friend represented the critical voice in my head, which was trying to tell me something important. I also realized that the baby was me, and that what I had forgotten in preparing for the women's conference was self-care. I had worked myself ragged and, sure enough, the day before the conference began, I came down with a bad cold.

Over the course of the conference, though I was still quite busy, I had to step back from doing some of the things I had expected to do. Traditionally, the co-clerks of the planning committee serve as emcees for the conference, and I did do that, introducing speakers for the plenaries and keeping everyone informed of what we would be doing next. My co-clerk and I were also the ones that everyone came to first with any problems that arose, so I did a lot of problem-solving. But I am grateful to my elders there (both official and unofficial) for keeping me from overdoing it. Ann, one of my designated elders, gently asked me whether I really felt led to speak on a panel (I did not), and another Friend suggested that it might be better for me to spend the time sleeping instead of going to early morning worship every day.

Elders have been essential in keeping me grounded and supporting me as I attempt to be faithful in ministry. An elder is someone who holds a minister and those gathered in prayer and helps to create space for the minister to deliver the message. I have also served as an elder for other ministers (I often say that I feel like I am about 75% minister and 25% elder) so I have experience both in working with elders as a minister and working with ministers as an elder. The roles are different, but both are based on listening to God and to others and responding as I feel led by the Spirit. My experience as an elder has made me very specific about what I want when someone serves as my elder.

Because elders and eldering have been so important to me, I have been surprised by the amount of resistance to the concept I have encountered among Friends. In some cases, this is a lack of knowledge of Friends' tradition of having elders. I have had Friends say to me that they didn't know that having someone upholding a minister or a gathering in prayer was a job. In other cases, however, people know what elders are and are resistant to the concept. Part of this may be history of abuse by elders (both personal and as a religious society), but I think it is also because our culture is so individualistic.

Despite our testimony of community, this is especially true for many

Friends. As Sue Gardner observed when she was learning about Quaker business process, Friends "have a strong individualistic streak, and describe themselves as skeptical about leadership and authority." Even though many of us know we desperately need support and accountability, Friends also struggle with the idea of submitting to another person's judgment.

Eldering is a spiritual gift that some people come by naturally, but it also involves a set of skills that an individual can learn and grow through practice and from others who are engaged in this work. Similarly, eldering can be done well or badly, and it is important to not take one example of bad eldering to say that eldering itself is bad. A gifted elder is a gifted listener—someone who can listen to the Spirit and the minister as well as those gathered, and provide guidance based on what she hears.

Two years after finishing my term as co-clerk, I returned to the women's conference. I was not on the planning committee for the 2012 conference, but I was asked to speak in one of the plenaries. I asked Ann to elder for me again. I knew this message would be a big one for me, and I wanted an elder who knew me well and whom I could trust to keep me grounded.

Before the conference, Ann and I emailed back and forth about what I needed in terms of support. During that time, I spent a lot of time in prayer about what I would need. I also thought about what I knew about the women's conference. In previous experiences of doing ministry, I had learned through a lot of trial and error what kind of support was essential for me, as well as what was helpful.

In an email to Ann, I briefly described the schedule for the plenary: I would have an hour to give a message out of worship, followed by a break, and then my co-presenter would lead an activity until it was time for lunch. I said that I would like to meet for worship before the plenary, and that I wanted her to sit near me when I spoke and to hold me in prayer. During the break, I asked that she make sure that I was eating a snack and drinking water, and, if possible, that she keep people away from me. I also asked her to walk me to lunch. And finally, I wanted to meet at some point later to debrief about the plenary.

Even though Ann is a dear friend, I was nervous sending the email. It is hard to ask for what I need! But Ann responded that she was touched and impressed that I had thought it through so carefully.

Then, one week before the women's conference, I got another cold. It was bad enough that I took a sick day from work. I stayed home wondering if I had strep throat and feeling sorry for myself. This was not how I wanted things to go. I had hoped to come to the conference feeling strong and well-rested; at that point, it seemed like the most I could hope for was to not have to interrupt my plenary by blowing my nose repeatedly.

As feeling sorry for myself got boring, I began to think about what I did want the plenary to be like. I knew that I wanted it to feel like worship, but I wasn't sure how to make that happen. I realized that the best way would be to ask weighty Friends to help ground the space, so I sent out an email to several Friends (of all ages) who I knew would be there. I said that I hoped the plenary would truly be a time of worship, and asked them to intentionally hold the gathering in prayer, especially as I began to speak. Over the next several hours, I heard back from almost everyone I included in the email. They said that they were happy to help ground the worship, and their responses made me feel supported and held.

The women's conference began on a Wednesday evening. By the time I met with Ann that night, I was feeling pretty scattered. I had worked a full day before getting a ride to the conference center with a woman I had never met, and in the last few miles of the drive, we got lost. We arrived late and snuck into the meeting room while the co-clerks were making announcements and introductions. Then we had the first meeting of our home groups—the small groups we would meet with throughout the conference. Ann and I didn't have time to get together until after 9:30pm. I was tired and irritable and not at all centered.

Fortunately, Ann is a very grounding person. She listened to me as I told her how I was feeling and what my hopes were for the plenary, which would take place the next morning. Then she said, "You are going to early worship, so I think you will be grounded by the time you are supposed to speak." Just hearing her say that was incredibly helpful. Ann also asked what I meant when I asked her to keep others away from me after I spoke. I said that, in my experience, people want to interact with me after I give a message, which is just when I am feeling most tired and vulnerable. Ann said that I might say something about that at the end of speaking, and we planned to go to another room, away from people, during the break.

We went together into the room where I would speak and started talking about moving the furniture. The podium was so large that I could barely see over it, so we found another one. We talked about how I would need water and agreed that someone else should close worship. The chairs were in rows instead of circles, so we planned to ask others to help us move them in the morning. Ann asked if I wanted her to go to early worship with me, and I said I did. She commented, "This eldering is a funny thing. It's half spiritual and half really practical!" We both went to bed after I promised to do my best to sleep and eat some breakfast.

The next morning, the plenary began with announcements and music. Then one of the co-clerks introduced me and we settled into open worship. I sat in worship, waiting for the message. Even though I had spent a lot of time over the weeks leading up to the conference writing out my notes and planning what I was going to say, I have given vocal ministry enough times to know I have to wait for the prompting of the Spirit to speak. I was prepared to sit for an hour of open worship if I did not feel that inner prompting. So we sat for a minute and then two, and people began to settle. After ten minutes, the room shifted, deepening. I finally felt the leading to stand, so I did, and delivered the message.

After I spoke, we settled back into open worship for about twenty minutes. As one of the co-clerks closed worship, I asked if I could say something. I went back to the microphone and said that although there were many Friends there that I wanted to connect with, I was feeling very tired and vulnerable, and so I asked everyone to give me some space until lunch. Then Ann and I went to another room, where I devoured a snack, drank lots of water, and we talked and sat together until lunchtime.

That afternoon, I crashed. I realized that I had been going from one thing to the next since the World Conference of Friends in Kenya two months before (and really, before that too). The message at the women's conference was the last thing I had to prepare for, and after finishing it, I suddenly felt the full impact of how exhausted I really was. In addition, I am an introvert. I find groups of people draining. Even though I wanted to connect with many of the conference attenders, I needed lots of space and time to myself.

So I cut back on what I was planning to do during the conference, and then I cut back some more. I went to bed early. I didn't go to any of the workshops. I found meals especially challenging. The dining hall was loud and it is hard for me to keep up a conversation while eating, so at one point, I asked Ann to sit next to me and not talk to me while I ate. She was happy to do so. I took naps and listened to music on my iPod and spent a lot of time lying in the grass, looking up at the clouds. I was grateful for the space that others had given me and grateful that, if I was going to run out of steam so completely, I could do it in such a beautiful setting. Slowly, I began to put myself back together again.

A few days later, after the conference ended, I had another vivid dream. In this dream, I was back at the women's conference, again talking with a friend. Suddenly, there was a commotion outside. We went out to see what was going on, and saw that there was a woman up on a high structure. All of the women below were worried about the safety of the woman above, but she didn't seem concerned. Then someone said, "Where is the baby?" We all anxiously looked around for the baby, when a woman standing nearby said, "I have her!" I looked over and saw that the baby was safely in that woman's arms. The baby was fat and happy, dressed, and oblivious to the drama going on around her. The baby was just fine.

LISTENING WITH OTHERS:
ACCOMPANIMENT IN MINISTRY

Christine Betz Hall

Fan into Flame of the Gift of God!

-2 Timothy 1:6

"WHO, ME?" used to be my first response to the possibility that my
gifts were meant to serve others somehow—that I might be called
to "minister." It's the Friends who walked beside faithfully as elders
who helped me say, "Yes! I'll do it." I'd start out with *who-me*-surprise,
add a natural shyness, and could have easily buried God's call under a
deep sense of my own inadequacies. Now I can laugh with my friend
and frequent elder, Cathy Walling, as I notice less need for "intensive
care" or "life support" in ministry. Still, I continue to learn from
the wisdom of the minister-elder dynamic. At first, I didn't know
what I needed to be faithful; now I wouldn't do without the formal
accompaniment that blesses the service I offer. My Quaker mentors,
whether in formal eldering roles, on support committees, or through
informal spiritual friendships, have been absolutely necessary to the
Right unfolding of any work of the Spirit I've taken up. They "fan the
flames" of the Gift in me.

I am extraordinarily grateful for a Quaker support committee
from my monthly meeting in Fairbanks, Alaska, that carried me
through five years of graduate theology studies and the beginnings
of ministry. Cathy began with me there, and continued to nurture,
affirm and support me as elder for my retreat facilitation and the
development of the Way of the Spirit retreat-study program on the

West Coast. Since 2010, when I moved to the Seattle area, an anchor committee through Port Townsend Monthly Meeting and Whidbey Island Friends Meeting has upheld me in ministry. I carry a letter of introduction from Whidbey Island Friends, and am an Associate with Good News Associates, a ministry cooperative that aids in discernment and offers financial accountability. I also accompany others as a spiritual director, a retreat leader, and adjunct professor at Seattle University's School of Theology and Ministry. So you see, I write from experience of the gracious gifts of God walking with others as minister, elder, and Friend.

Opening Up to Accompaniment

But I wasn't so enthusiastic about eldering when I began my Quaker journey. Like many contemporary Quakers in the unprogrammed worshipping tradition, deep-rooted individualism increased my resistance to others' help and support. But I trusted the first Friend who gently suggested that a support committee might be appropriate as I began studies in theology and spiritual care. I remembered how useful clearness committees had been at crucial moments in my life. And I knew this Friend appreciated my commitment to and struggle with faithfulness. So in her suggestion I sensed an intriguing spiritual invitation into something new, something I didn't yet see the value of... but it couldn't hurt, right?

In the beginning, eldering support helped heal the timid places in me, build my confidence, and liberate the Love that I am meant to offer others. I tip too easily toward fear with an inner voice that says, "I don't know what to say!" or "They won't like me." I learned how fear hinders the work of the Spirit; it hampers my willingness to step into unfamiliar leadership roles, closes my heart to the Spirit's nudges during ministry, and cuts off my sense of the condition of others whose souls I'm called to tend.

Some of the best early eldering support I received was after public ministry. Leadership roles can exhaust me; that fatigue sparks an over-active inner critic that can cast me into discouragement about where I faltered, or when I missed cues for where Spirit was trying to lead. An elder helps me evaluate what had happened in a more balanced way—celebrating the affirmations and listening carefully for hints of what the Inward Teacher might say about where I need to grow.

Elders also ask intriguing questions. At the end of one retreat I led, I was checking in with my elder. As I shared my joy and appreciation for the participants, and my sense of alignment with them and the Spirit's movements among us, she noted my excitement and asked, "What does it take to get you to this place?" "A weekend on retreat!" I answered instantly. That simple query guided my preparations for later retreats to include a day in prayerful preparation. Gentle care in debriefing makes it possible for me to continue to learn and grow in the work before me.

The Discipline of Humility

I'm learning that Spirit-led service has its hazards. Some are unique to my background and gifts; others fall into recognizable patterns according to my temperament or the communities I serve. With accompaniment, I chart internal obstacles, discern my accountability, and avoid burnout. The process invites me to humility—an old word. I aim for humility as a spiritual discipline—cultivating openness to being teachable, an expectation that God's guidance may come through another's words even if they challenge me. I realize I am less faithful when I avoid listening to those who may "see" something I do not, or when I assume my perspective is already complete. The humorous scriptural tale of the prophet Balaam and his talking donkey illustrates and guides me here (Numbers 22:21-35). Balaam's humble pack animal sees the angel of God blocking the path forward, while the mighty prophet remains blind and bitterly beats the donkey.

When elders or a support committee "test" my sense of leading, it can feel confrontational. Like Balaam's response to his donkey, I can feel impatient and angry at perceived interference with "my" mission. But Balaam's donkey, like any good support staff, talks back and questions even when it's inconvenient and embarrassing to the prophet. The work of God, distinct from what the prophet thought that mission should be, could have failed without the donkey's actions. God needs both prophets and donkeys. Can I, a modern, individualistic would-be prophet, learn from Balaam to remain humbly open to correction? Who can correct me and how?

The best elders have raised awareness of my growing edges in ministry even during an event I'm facilitating. Once on retreat, Cathy was sitting next to me during an energetic group discussion. Her posture is usually prayerful, eyes closed. She rarely speaks, but tells me she is sensing and upholding the condition of me and the group. Thirty people were considering the centrality of the "gathered" meeting in Quaker experience. Questions were flying, since most of the group hadn't explored the concept, or didn't know how to connect their experience to the Quaker heritage. My mind was racing. My words were coming fast. I wanted to answer all these ideas, and felt a challenging edge to my voice. Cathy leaned over, put her hand on my knee, and quietly stopped me with the clear and concise observation that I was not letting people finish their thoughts. I was interrupting!

I wrote later that I'd not only come up to my growing edge…

> "I almost jumped off a cliff…. It wasn't just tiptoeing to the precipice,
> I was taking a flying leap into the air and Cathy yanked me back. I say
> 'yanked' because the intervention felt so utterly abrupt to me. And
> completely necessary. At first, I felt criticized, then ashamed of myself.
> She caught that shift in energy too, and said she hoped I didn't take that
> as criticism. She deftly turned me aside from another cliff edge: ego-
> mangling self denigration. Right. Not helpful right then. My thoughts
> slowed. My inner orientation shifted back to God. I prayed a quiet, little,
> "Help! What is needed now?" Some clarity emerged: Not notions, not
> ideas… listening… care and gratitude for these people. It's not about
> me. When we reconvened after a short break, I slowed the pace of the
> interchange, made sure to let people finish their thoughts and thanked
> them. As I was listening to them, I was not thinking of what to say next. I
> was attending to them, focused and appreciative, prayerful for and about
> them, welcoming them inwardly. A contemplative stance, I see now.
>
> Through the day, I reflected on that shift from ideas and answers to
> gratitude. Gratitude is one of my core spiritual practices. It calls me out
> of my own head, and out of my self-doubt, into the moment and presence
> of the people God wishes to touch through me. This is important."

Some may imagine that this kind of accompaniment is too intrusive. But I can attest "by the fruits" to its benefits—growth in my ability to act in love, a settled peace with the outcome, and joy in being corrected before I might have unknowingly disappointed others who were only seeking understanding and Grace.

I wonder about the kind of submission that seems required of a minister during accompaniment. Do I do everything my elder says? No. This humility is not blind obedience. At least once, I have dismissed an elder's words as contrary to true leading.

Listening and Testing

As I attempt to act faithfully, I lean on Divine guidance in and through both myself and my elder. Usually, when I pause and reflect, the elder's guidance is confirmed within me with an inner, "Oh, I see," or "Of course." I am prone to rush "ahead of the Guide," as early Quakers said, and eldering slows me down. How do I discern what is of the Spirit, and what is irrelevant to a task in its specific time and place? With a little time, I can probe inwardly in prayer; I notice possible next steps and poke at alternatives until one has a kind of spiritual softness, or give. I sense something like way opening into Grace. Less helpful options have a hardness or impenetrability about them, as odd as that sounds. How can I best hear correction from an elder? I appreciate a gentle delivery, but expect candor. An elder's words boost me forward in faithfulness, without shutting me down emotionally or spiritually. More than anything, I must be able to trust an elder's spiritual discernment, which springs from a devoted and joyous prayer life.

I am less faithful, or less available for God's work in and through me when my inner motives tend toward self-sufficiency—when I expect the Spirit's help in ways "I" think of, or I have "something to prove," or I attempt to cover up my own errors or failings, or act as if "I" have to bring everything this group needs. I have learned to trust that creative Spirit to use other wisdom in the room to fill in the gaps of my presentation or fumbling words. I feel great freedom in not bearing sole responsibility for what happens. The give and take of the minister-elder relationship, honest dialogue, and prayerful listening to God provides more channels for the Living Water than my limited vessel. That abundant Life and Power seems to seek out any conduit to which I'll pay attention.

When I am working with an elder, I like to have her or him sitting near me in the circle. I might lean over to consider timing for an unexpected break, or gauge how a session is unfolding while the group engages in separate sharing. On lengthy retreats, I check in privately every day. We reflect on the group's and my spiritual condition, consider our sense of the group's needs, and discuss any distractions or outright conflicts. The elder usually asks after my sleep and spiritual renewal or down time. Before a recent retreat, I warned the elder, Eugene Norcross-Renner, that I suspected I'd have trouble with too much content in the schedule; I'd sensed an unhelpful attachment to the content in my reluctance to let anything go. During the retreat Eugene helped me filter ego needs and better focus on the group's condition. He affirmed when to drop an entire session, and shift into silence. His clarity confirmed the hints of the Inner Teacher's guidance when I might have blundered onward with the best intentions, but little Light.

Tuning Inward, Tuning Outward

Recently I was confused, and consulted several wise Quaker elders. I'd begun teaching in a graduate theology and ministry program, and inwardly struggled with the differences between soul-nurturing and teaching. As a spiritual director/guide or retreat leader, I'd developed a prayerful attentiveness to the tone, energy, connections between, and responses of others. In those eldering roles, when I nurture, affirm and support another person or group, I intentionally hone this sensitivity to serve them. All my intuitive people-reading skills are on high alert.

By contrast, as a teacher, or a minister with a message, I've needed an inward personal attentiveness that allows me to speak authentically, with confidence and joy as the Spirit guides. I still care for others, and pray my words resound with God's compassion for their needs. But outward observations can distract me, hinder my ability to speak the language of Truth and Power that rises from within. Usually the distraction sounds like a snide little voice in my head saying, "They don't respect you," or "You're doing it wrong." Maybe you hear echoes of your own demons. One Quaker friend articulated this unusual situation as having one person serving two functions: both minister and elder. I'm learning the inner realities and challenges of shifting between those functions. When one function comes forward, the other may need to recede. So I'm tuning down my people-antennae to free the messages God wants me to share.

Seeking Eldering from the Community

Complementing one-to-one minister-elder relationships, I depend on an anchor or support committee through my home Quaker community. Two groups of Friends have discerned way forward for me in ministry over the past eight years, appointed by ministry and council committees in two monthly meetings. Our current format feels like the best of Quaker clearness process. We are guided by a School of the Spirit Ministry publication offering helpful definitions and advice for committee members and those following their leadings. Our mutual accountability is first of all to God's guidance and "whether [I] am making right use of [my] gifts in the service of God and God's beloved."

The committee witnesses to my public ministry with regular reports to the business session, an ongoing accountability to the larger body of Friends. They connect me to my spiritual "home," and like an anchor, prevent me from drifting in the wind or current. My monthly meeting has not sought clearness to endorse or formally record what I do, so the anchor committee doesn't supervise so much as discern and pray with me. I write regular reflections for them about my work and spiritual condition. A few important queries frame my writing and sharing: How have I been faithful? What challenges or blocks did I face? How did I meet them? What did I learn this month? What is God calling forth in me? How can the committee be helpful? Preparing these reports helps me articulate my life in ministry with integrity. The committee is one tool for continuing unfolding of my work, and I am deeply grateful for their care.

Over the years, I've also compiled wisdom gleaned through accompaniment into a personal ministry journal. Through these pages I continue to hear the voices of the people who have helped free and shape the ministry in me. Once when traveling in ministry without pre-arranged eldering, I felt a bit unmoored from my usual supports. An hour's review of my journal restored my balance and openness to the movements of the Spirit. Then in a trusting frame of mind, I sat down to dinner next to a woman who became the perfect elder for the next day's plenary. From the start, I've kept a list of "affirmations," since I quickly forget the sense of rightness and joy that sweeps me along in ministry. Other pages capture my learnings on discernment, discouragement, evaluating the ministry, images of Quaker leadership, sense of self and God in ministry, quotes and scripture on a variety of topics including calling, voice, and leadership, and much more. The journal is precious to me.

Many Friends describe eldering through the metaphor of midwifery. I've come to experience God's good and holy work as a Gift seeking to be born through me. As in childbirth, sometimes in ministry I've needed I to give myself over to the powerful process; I needed support to shed my fears and self-centered protections. Yes, birthing is painful, but resistance hurts too. And when it's time, an elder reminds me I need to *push*. Ministry requires my intense engagement in the moment. There's a lovely irony here. Infertility stole my ability to birth children, but I am blessed to use this metaphor freely, and find great joy in a vicarious birth experience in ministry. The beginning of the Way of the Spirit program in 2012 was such a birth, and seemed to more than make up for my loss. I rely on midwives to both guide and correct the birthing process. In turn, I serve as midwife to the spiritual births of others for the building up of God's Peaceable Realm. May we continue to be faithful together.

Discerning

Ann Stever &
Dorsey Green
Nancy Irving
Neal Andrews
Nancy Thomas
Eleanor Dart
C. Wess Daniels

I T'S ONE THING to have faith that God, Jesus, Spirit, the Divine, can speak to you, or to anyone who does the hard work of careful listening for the still, small voice of God. It is another thing entirely to be able to tell when it is in fact divine guidance, and when it is human ego. The work of discerning if and where that divine guidance is present is carried out both corporately and as individuals.

Those who are new to Friends—and some of those of us who are well-acquainted—are frequently thunderstruck by the thoughtfulness and care for one another that is exhibited when Friends are making decisions. Often mistaken (even by Friends) as consensus, the traditional practice is instead much harder and more complex. It is often called "seeking the sense of the Meeting." In his Pendle Hill pamphlet, *Beyond Consensus: Salvaging the Sense of the Meeting*, Friend Barry Morley describes it beautifully:

> When we seek the sense of the meeting we allow ourselves to be directed to the solution that awaits us. It is a process of surrender to our highest natures, and a recognition that, even though each of us is posessed of light, there is only one Light. At the end of the process we reside in that Light. We have allowed ourselves to be led to a transcendent place of unmistakable harmony, peace, and tender love.

It must be said that newcomers and seasoned Friends alike are in equal numbers irritated when, as so often happens, a group of Quakers falls short of this worshipful state, and dissolves into nitpicking and self-interested grandstanding. This is one of the difficulties of being part of a mystical, seeking, faith tradition; when working with a group, the ability to transcend our frailties rests equally on everyone's shoulders. It's unlikely that everyone gathered at a given time is fully up to the difficult work of centering down, listening for the collective wisdom and divine guidance, and making their personal desires secondary. That's where leadership comes in, as Ann and Dorsey explain so well at the beginning of this section. Nancy Irving speaks to another important aspect of leadership and discernment: that in a Quaker context, where leadership roles rotate through the community, we are always engaged in nurturing leadership through our friendships, our discussions and the small things that make up relationships. She also addresses the challenges of formulating quick but discerning responses to situations.

Early Friends sought to live their lives according to their Guide as much as they could. Many Friends today also seek to cultivate that depth of connection to the Spirit; it's a theme that arises over and over in this book. Discernment in this context can look a little different. Sometimes there's big stuff that really requires airing with others, and sometimes there are little nudges in a particular direction. Interesting things happen in your life when you follow those nudges, as Nancy Thomas relates in her story about using a listening stick during a workshop. And sometimes it's not a nudge so much as it is a clarion call to a particular action, as Eleanor experienced with her leading to become a civilian counselor with the military. In these instances, group discernment can prove challenging. In the section on Leadership in Quaker Organizations, you'll hear more about Friends' history of individuals who discern an individual call that others in their Quaker community do not. Every society, even the Society of Friends, needs its boat-rockers and rabble-rousers to keep the discomforts of a less-than-ideal reflection always in plain view in the proverbial mirror. But as Neal attests to in his essay, being a faithful boat-rocker when you are also an elected official is hard, and keeping your discernment process simple does not make it easy.

Finally, Wess looks at the gap between our everyday reality and what is possible—a space that Quaker educator Parker Palmer has named "the tragic gap." Discernment is an essential tool for navigating that gap with grace. It opens us up to compassion and empathy for those different from us, and fans the flames of hope as we navigate the tensions of daily life.

Queries on Discerning

Ann and Dorsey describe discernment as "the practice of listening to both the human voices and Divine, sifting the wheat from the chaff, and holding it all in the Light to be able to find where we are led as a group." How might you contribute to this process? Can you identify things you might do that would detract from it?

Have you ever felt a "nudge," an impulse to do something that seems to come from someplace beyond yourself? How did you respond, and what happened?

When you are in a leadership position, what do you do to prepare yourself to lead?

What gives you strength in times of conflict?

Discernment often leads to an unexpected outcome. Are you open to that sort of unpredictable possibility? What can you do to build your trust in God, yourself, and others? How does this relate to discernment?

SIFTING THE WHEAT FROM THE CHAFF: CLERKS, DISCERNMENT, AND QUAKER DECISION-MAKING

Ann Stever and Dorsey Green

L EADERSHIP AMONG FRIENDS begins with God, the Divine, the Spirit, that which is beyond and among us all. When we talk about human leadership and Friends, we first need to acknowledge that people are given different gifts and that a variety of gifts are crucial to a healthy, well-functioning monthly meeting or church. A leader uses his or her own gifts, but also recognizes the gifts of the members and asks for help from them, as well as from the Divine.

How these gifts are called upon by the community is an important part of understanding the Quaker decision-making process. We acknowledge with appreciation the pastors and behind-the-scenes leaders who are also part of the leadership of Quaker meetings and churches. However, our focus here is on the job of the clerks, the servant-leaders of our business meetings and committees.

The Language of Discernment

Decision-making among Quakers is a distinctive, unusual, and sometimes frustrating process, particularly for those new to Friends. Simply put, those gathered at a Meeting for Worship for the Purpose of Business are looking for, or discerning, a sense of the meeting— God's will for this group, on this topic, at this time. But there are important limitations to note. Quakers do not claim to know God's will for everyone on all issues for all time. Rather, because a basic premise of Quakerism is that each individual has the capacity to have a direct, unmediated experience of God, we have found that when we are gathered together, the accumulated experience of the Divine is more likely to find where the Spirit is leading us. We are making a decision with the Light that we are given at that time. This leaves open the possibility for another decision at another time—given new Light. The Light, or Inward Light, "refers to the presence of God in our hearts and lives, a reality which guides and directs us, which gives us strength to act on this guidance, and thus brings us into unity with the Spirit of God" (from the glossary of *Faith & Practice of North Pacific Yearly Meeting of the Religious Society of Friends.*)

Discernment is the practice of listening to both the human voices and divine, sifting the wheat from the chaff, and holding it all in the Light to be able to find where we are led as a group. Often, in a gathered Meeting for Business, where those present feel a strong presence of the Spirit, the meeting unites in a decision that no one predicted. It feels like something bigger than all of us is holding and helping us move to a deep sense of rightness. This sense of rightness is present only when all members of the meeting are able to say 'we,' not 'they' made this decision.

Friends use the terms 'sense of the meeting' or 'unity.' They are similar to consensus, yet very different. Groups that use consensus are looking for a decision that everyone can agree with. It often involves considerable compromise. As Friends do in seeking a sense of the meeting, consensus participants are expected to listen, speak for themselves only, and discuss the ideas presented in respectful ways. The primary difference is that when Quakers are seeking unity, we are purposefully listening for a leading or voice, if you will, that is not human. It is the Light that leads us to a place that is right for the group, not just a decision that everyone can agree to.

Light can come through anyone present, even a first-time attender at a business meeting. We like the image someone gave us that a decision may end up being only point A on the way to point D but you had to get to A to be able to see the way clear to D. The community can only go as far as it is led and can discern.

Discernment and Disagreement

Sometimes Friends and others believe that unity or sense of the meeting means all those present have to agree with a decision before it can be approved. While that is ideal, it is not uncommon for a business meeting to move ahead even when someone in the group disagrees and wants to prevent the action. In this case, provided the Friend's objections seem to come from a spiritual as well as experiential depth, the group may delay the decision for a month—or even years— as in the case of early American Friends' decisions about slavery. Modern Friends meetings have waited as long as ten years before approving minutes supporting same-sex marriage in their meeting.

During the month or years of seasoning, everyone in the meeting is charged with talking and listening to Friends with whom they disagree. Everyone is encouraged to learn in as many ways as possible about the matter at hand. However, in the end, it is only the Spirit of Truth as perceived by the corporate group that can 'stand in the way of' or obstruct an action.

One of the beauties of the process is that one person can indeed be given the Light that changes a whole group. Many years ago a board member of the American Friends Service Committee (AFSC) 'held up' (delayed) a decision to nominate Caesar Chavez for the Nobel Peace Prize. The individual had experience working with farmworkers and was aware of the United Farm Worker's (Chavez's group at the time) policy of threatening undocumented strikebreakers with a call to the Immigration Service. He felt the policy was a violent one.

As a result, the board delayed their decision and studied the situation, initiating discussions with Chavez and others. AFSC recognized that the state of affairs was pitting the poor (UFW) against the poor (undocumented workers) for the crumbs from the table. The AFSC then developed a program that lasted for decades, dealing with the full range of problems related to the U.S.-Mexico border. The board was very clear that this one Friend was led by the Spirit to show the organization where it should go. At the same time and having gained a greater understanding, it was also clear, with the agreement of the one Friend, to go ahead with the Chavez nomination.

Friends' discernment process works well for setting policy and major decisions in Quaker meetings and organizations. An individual, designated committee, or small group is best for straightforward decisions such as a color of paint for the walls.

The Role of the Clerk

There are many components that contribute to successful decision-making and implementation in business meeting. Good spiritual practice is wonderful, but without organization and action it remains just good spiritual practice. When all these elements are combined, Quakers can be a notable and extraordinary force in the world.

We believe strongly that clerks need to love their meetings or churches; it takes a loving heart to hold the group tenderly when we are wrestling with the mundane or the profound. A clerk is seen as a Friend who has a demonstrated ability to listen deeply to all the human voices, as well as that of the Divine, to sort out the threads of what is being said, and to offer them to the body for reflection and discernment.

This Friend must be spiritually centered for business meeting, and also prepare in some very concrete ways. S/he gathers the material that is to be presented and considered by the meeting, organizes the agenda, and ensures the presenters have all the information needed to help the meeting make a decision, as well as ascertaining how much time the presenters will need. The clerk may need to coach an inexperienced presenter. If an item on the agenda is part of ongoing discernment, the clerk should be sure that any who have been given specific assignments (e.g. gathering information) have done their job and are prepared to present this work.

The clerk sometimes takes on a pastoral job of listening. When Dorsey became clerk of University Meeting, the meeting had been struggling with the issue of same-sex marriage. She visited, one-on-one, the relatively small number of vocal opponents and listened to their questions, concerns, and opinions. It is possible that this act opened the way for the community to come to a decision to perform same-sex marriages in the meeting. That decision was made in an extraordinary meeting in which one Friend said: "I felt the Spirit creeping into my toes, then filling my body, then filling the room, then filling our whole community of people who were not present." The next day the Friends who had been identified as opponents were called. The response of one was similar to all: "I don't know if I will understand this, but I am so glad the Meeting has come to unity." This is the essence of a Friends process, and of one aspect of leadership among Friends.

Clerks have the responsibility of keeping the Meeting for Business as safe as possible for participants. Among other things, this means reminding Friends of 'good order'—to ask for the clerk's recognition before speaking, address the clerk, not another meeting member, and to speak only once on any given topic unless given new light to offer. (There is an exception for someone saying they have changed their mind. That can be a real gift to a meeting.)

Sometimes Quakers can confuse an open seeking of the Spirit with a lack of behavioral guidelines. The absence of good order can in fact shut down the Spirit. Friends become tense, unable to relax into worship, and wary of speaking for fear of someone's judgment. This robs the Meeting for Business of needed Light. When we clerk, we like to present some of the good practice guidelines at the beginning of each meeting to remind Friends of our responsibility to behave well.

It is the clerk's job to discern and articulate the sense of the meeting. This job combines head, heart, and spiritual sensitivity. Sometimes the clerk will need to 'test' whether the meeting is close to unity by suggesting a solution may be at hand. This process helps a meeting know where it is. It is important that the clerk understands s/he does not have to get it right. In fact, getting it wrong and being gently corrected by Friends can move the meeting forward. It reminds everyone we are all in this together, all responsible to the Spirit.

Humility and resilience are both important qualities for a clerk. We all learn by doing and from our mistakes as well as 'successes'–the greatest success being when we have gotten out of the way and let the Spirit lead the group. All clerks should have 'elders' or a few people they trust to hold them in the Light during the meeting as well as to debrief with afterward. They can help the clerk better learn how to encourage Spirit-led guidance the next time around.

Clerks come in many flavors. Some are gifted at holding the center of the worship in a business meeting, so that Friends can almost see the Spirit flowing through that person into the room. Some are gifted at instinctively knowing which person can offer the needed words in a discernment process. Some are gifted in framing the words for an eloquent minute. Some are gifted in organization, tracking details and supporting Friends who have jobs to do. Some are gifted in their sense of ease and humor. Some are gifted in being fresh and innovative, others in being deeply experienced elders. The meeting that thrives can maximize the gifts of any given clerk and can support him or her in the areas where s/he is not strong. While the clerk is indeed a leader, the clerk is not alone and depends on the strengths of those in the Meeting and his/ her depth of connection with the Spirit. Our own experiences of clerking have been blessed times of spiritual growth and supportive love from our human community.

SEEKING DIVINE WISDOM

Nancy Irving

E VERY ORGANIZATION, including the Religious Society of Friends, needs leaders. They will emerge even when the system calls for a level playing field such as ours does. In fact, it is part of the work of a worshipping community to identify gifts that each member brings to the whole, and leadership is one of them. Our gifts grow and develop and even atrophy over time, so that means that someone is not a clerk for life any more than someone is a greeter at the door for life. Leaders do not necessarily have a more direct line to the Divine than others; rather they bring to the community the gift of helping manifest that Divine wisdom and guidance the group has discerned.

Learning in Community

Lifelong organizing skills evolved into leadership skills over the course of many years in my life. My consciousness of my own spiritual journey and development was interwoven into that evolution. Spiritual joys and discoveries as well as dark times are all part of leadership development in my experience. I am grateful that I had role models and places where I was encouraged to 'try my wings' in different situations.

When I was 25, I found myself in tandem situations that have shaped how I lead. One was within my Meeting and the other in my work life in the business world. There were many parallels which reinforced lessons that I learned.

I took a job with a company that provided the headquarters for national business trade associations. I started out as an administrative assistant to a senior executive named Bruce Wall. We were a team of three: Bruce, our secretary Pat (straight out of parochial school) and me. As I came to appreciate, Bruce's attitude was that it was in his own best interests for Pat and me to know everything he knew (with a few limitations). There was none of the "I'm your boss, so I control the information" game. Likewise, we shared with him what we learned. We wanted him to be successful, and he wanted us all to fully serve our clients. It was the most ideal work situation I could have had. In turn, he recognized my skills and saw to it that I got promoted even when it meant losing me on his team (and me losing him). Bruce was a devout Presbyterian who walked his talk, and he was a good role model for me.

About the same time, I was attending a large urban Meeting. One Sunday there was an announcement that a discussion group on feminism would begin Monday evening. I went. It was a fairly large group, and it became apparent that there was a great variety of interests and goals. Meeting weekly, we threshed though all the personal agendas and agreed upon a creative listening process with shared leadership. Each week's designated leader was responsible for bringing a query or exercise.

Over time, we ranged way beyond feminism. The group continued to meet weekly except in the summers for six years. With deepening love and trust, we shared each other's birthdays, weddings, births, crises, and sorrows. We also shared our love for our Meeting, and each in our own way became deeply involved. I think because there was this core group who knew me well, I plugged into the Meeting's committees at a younger age than is usual today. I recollect I became Clerk of Worship & Ministry while in my early 30's and also served as an Overseer after having clerked another committee—all before I moved away at age 35.

In both my meeting life and my work life, I was dealing with groups of people, committees, minutes, and visioning. I developed a sense of how to separate wheat from chaff in various environments. I learned about priorities. In neither situation could I be a 'boss;' I was always in service to the group. Even in later work situations where I *was* the boss, I continued to adopt the attitude of service despite my role as final decision-maker.

Finding a Way Forward

Beyond my local Meeting, my yearly meeting asked me to serve as one of its representatives to the Friends World Committee for Consultation—in essence to be a member of a committee of 300-plus members from each of the yearly meetings around the world. Yearly meetings are the organizational structure that the local meetings belong to—often they are national or, in the case of the United States, Kenya, India, Burundi and Bolivia, they are regional. Usually referred to as FWCC, this committee meets face to face every three or four years. FWCC itself is comprised of four autonomous regions called sections: the Americas, Europe & the Middle East, Africa, and Asia-West Pacific. The Section of the Americas has a representatives' meeting on an annual basis.

In the late 1990's, I served on the Executive Committee of the Friends World Committee Section of the Americas. Its function is to oversee and guide the work of the Section between the annual representatives' meetings. Needing some clarity on the way forward as we faced resource and financial challenges, we took a four-day retreat at a Quaker center in North Carolina and asked Laura Melly to facilitate our deliberations. She led us in a wide variety of exercises that helped us all find words to express our thoughts and feelings and eventually our vision for the Section. That newly-articulated vision reflected the organization and its current resources and prospects rather than a 'blue sky,' wishful-thinking vision. Then she had us apply our newly-found vision to our organization.

That was the real challenge. Led by our clerk (chair) Tom Hill, we looked at our many-faceted organization and had to acknowledge that some of the facets of our work did not mesh with our vision. We struggled with the prospect of letting go committees and groups the Section had initiated and fostered over many years and which in one case provided a part of the Section's revenue. As we moved forward in worship, we threshed and prayed and cried. It was not easy. Now, more than a decade later, we can look back and see that it was divinely led. We found homes for much of the work we laid down and, perhaps most dramatically, asked Right Sharing of World Resources to become an independent organization within the next few years. This came as a surprise to that committee and staff, but they accepted the challenge and today the organization has grown and thrived as an organization that promotes indigenous micro-credit groups in Kenya, India, and West Africa, in addition to encouraging North Americans to live more mindfully.

Discerning the Needs of the Whole

More recently, I was called to the position of General Secretary of Friends World Committee in the World Office in London. This role entails working with the four Sections, helping coordinate Quaker work at the United Nations, and representing Friends in ecumenical bodies of other Christian world communions. For nearly nine years until I retired, I travelled extensively among Friends, listening, observing, and linking Friends together. Since the tumultuous nineteenth century in which religious fervor in North America led to numerous schisms and divisions of Friends along theological lines, the world of Friends on all the continents has reflected these divisions. A major part of the work of FWCC is to serve as the place where the many varieties of Friends can come together to work together, make connections, and to honor our differences while acknowledging our kinship and common heritage. Its role is not to re-unite the factions but rather to respect each yearly meeting's theology.

As a leader of an international organization, namely the world-wide organization of all Friends, I lived with the daunting challenge of reflecting the needs of the whole, not just the groups that were very articulate. A case in point was the concern for the environment. The voices, emanating from several countries, were mostly liberal theologically and politically, and generally white. As Friends World Committee is the only organization which can issue statements in the name of *all* Friends and as Quaker work at the United Nations is done in the name of FWCC, there had been general minutes on the subject passed at our international meetings since the early 1990's. But as FWCC is consultative only, it could only transmit these minutes to the yearly meetings and encourage them to embrace the message and take action. This didn't satisfy the growing number of Friends expressing deeply-held concerns and leadings about the environment.

As General Secretary, I was being told that FWCC should, ought or must generally create a new committee or organization to advocate and coordinate change. This came at a time when FWCC was particularly resource-deficient and I was the only full-time employee, although I re-structured the staff to create another full-time post. Knowing what our vision was—and it is not to become a social action advocacy organization—and also aware that I wasn't hearing voices from other parts of the Quaker family, I was resisting these voices although I sympathized with them. How could FWCC respond to this global need and yet remain true to its calling? Even though the issue was and is global in its impact, we were not hearing the concern from other voices within the diverse array of Friends' traditions.

It came to a head at the November 2008 meeting of the FWCC representatives in the Asia-West Pacific Section in Bhopal, India, which only occurs every three years. It was also attended by the World Central Executive Committee (CEC) which held its annual meeting afterwards. Two members of the Section who were particularly strident on this issue asked to meet with me and Jocelyn Burnell, clerk of the CEC. Going into that meeting, Jocelyn and I separately prayed about it, carrying a concern and a lack of clarity about the way forward. In the course of the meeting, Jocelyn and I tried to articulate what FWCC was capable of doing and what it was not—in other words, the purpose of the organization and what was realistic to expect of it.

Then a phrase came to my mind out of my experience with the Quaker United Nations work: *convening authority*. Convening authority means that when a meeting is called, people will attend out of trust and respect for the organization. In the past, FWCC has convened consultations on such issues as identity and authority among Friends, not so much to find unity on the issue but to hear each others' experience. It hadn't been done since 1997, and then it was on a small, invitational basis involving less than 100 people.

So we talked about the idea of convening a consultation to incorporate the voices not being heard and to learn what is happening on the local level in different parts of the world. At their behest, the Asia/West Pacific Section approved a minute to the CEC requesting it consider convening a consultation on global change. The CEC had a lot of questions and concerns about the practicalities and formed an ad hoc feasibility committee to consider this and to report back at the next CEC meeting. We quickly formed an international committee which met only by telephone conference call. It recommended a grassroots consultation process centered around a set of six queries which would be the same world-wide, to be supplemented by a website for collecting the responses, to be followed by a consultation which would prepare a report for an upcoming 2012 worldwide conference of Friends. This Global Change Consultation Process was approved subject to fundraising among new donors, so as not to reduce contributions from donors that help keep the doors open. While it did not move ahead exactly as originally envisioned and fundraising proved difficult, the grassroots consultation process in local groups proceeded in Africa, Asia, and parts of Latin America, in addition to North America and Europe. That was perhaps the greatest gift of the process—that we heard for the first time voices which have never been heard or even consulted before. There was a global sense of participation and concern. The process ended in April 2012 as the World Conference issued the *Kabarak Call to Peace & Eco-Justice* (online at www.saltandlight2012.org.)

In hindsight, I am aware of the difficulties and shortcomings of the process, but it was ground-breaking in that we learned we could function in different ways, use technology, and be innovative—as well as move ahead on a shoestring! FWCC was able to stay true to its vision and purpose while providing a service no other organization could provide. Quakerism is a 'bottom-up' faith and it is appropriate that the major part of its work is conducted on a national or local level. I think that is what we strive for—a sense of leadership as service.

QUAKER SERVICE IN THE PUBLIC SPHERE

Neal Andrews

M Y MOTHER GAVE me the foundation upon which my leadership career has been built. She did it very carefully and deliberately. She was dying of cancer and knew she only had a limited amount of time, so she worked hard, I ultimately came to understand, to help develop in me the skills and self-confidence to succeed in life before she passed.

Her efforts were subtle but profound. When I was around five years of age, I was rambling about the house, getting underfoot, when Mother stopped what she was doing and asked if I would like to go play with my cousins, who lived about a mile and a half away. I thought that was a really keen idea, so off we went walking along the country road that would take us to my cousins' house. There were no sidewalks, but there was a well-worn path that ambled along the fields and woods beside the road, sometimes diverting deeper into the woods to avoid an obstacle. Every quarter mile or so the path would come to a "Y" where one fork would lead off in a different direction, either toward a farm house in the distance, or to some other destination.

As we walked that day, Mother took care to talk about the things we saw along the path. She pointed out the big oak tree that had been hit by lightning and had a burn scar in its trunk, and the small brook that ran beside the path for a little while. At every place where we had to make a choice about which direction to go, she would point out some landmark in the direction of our travel. She stopped to tell me about the white quartz vein that shone from the rock face of a ledge along the trail and how some people thought you would find gold if you dug around such a vein. I can't imagine any little boy with dreams of pirate's gold would ever forget such a thing.

By and by, we reached my cousins' home and I had a great time at play with my cousins while my mother and aunt chatted and worked at a quilt they were making together. On the trek home my mother and I had much the same conversation about all the sights we saw along the way.

About a week later, she asked me again if I would like to visit my cousins, and I was eager to do so. However, once I had stoked up my enthusiasm for the idea, she told me that she was not feeling so well after all. I made a fuss about not being able to go. Finally, she stopped what she was doing and quietly asked whether I thought I might be big enough to go alone.

Now, whoever heard of a five year old who would say he was not old enough to do something adventurous! As we discussed whether I was truly big enough to make the trek alone, she carefully mentioned all the sights we had noted before, in the order of their appearance. She never suggested that I should remember them or follow them, just casually spoke of them in a manner that reminded me of everything we had seen in the first walk.

When at last I convinced her that I remembered all that stuff and was surely old enough to go on my own without her, she set me off down the path. I had no difficulty finding my cousins' home, and we had great fun playing together that afternoon.

It was not until about thirty years later, long after my mother had passed, that my eldest brother told me the story about how Mother had made him follow me at a distance, to assure that I got there safely. It was her way of helping build independence and self-confidence in me. And, he noted, it was neither the first nor last time that she set me upon a course fraught with some modicum of risk and used my brothers to shadow me and assure my safety or success.

Mother also instilled in me the fundamental principles and precepts of my Quaker faith. She firmly believed that God was with us at all times and that we need only open to Him to know the Way.

(Her insurance program using my brother was simply a pragmatic acknowledgement that a five year old may not yet know how to open that relationship; truth be told I still find it challenging at nigh seventy years of age.)

For the last twelve years, I have served my community as an elected City Councilman representing a constituency of about 110,000 people. I have faced many challenges as I have attempted to maintain the principles of my faith and effectively lead in public office.

The most obvious challenge is with open testimony of my personal relationship with God as one with whom I communicate and who responds to me personally and individually. It is one thing for a minister or priest to assert that he or she thinks God has communicated to him or her, and quite another for a political leader to make such an assertion. In the first case, the reaction may be approval, benign interest, or mere skepticism, but in the latter it can range from ridicule to horror—or, conceivably, recall from office on grounds of mental incompetence.

When I look for Divine guidance in making difficult or weighty decisions for my community, I rarely share the process publicly. Sometimes I feel guilty about that, because my caution denies the public an opportunity to observe the Quaker way. It also deprives my faith community of an opportunity to be better understood and appreciated. But, I do believe it is an unfortunate but practical necessity of successful political life—one which places me in tension with the value Quakers place upon truth and integrity. Nonetheless, I learned a long time ago that not all truths need to be told.

An Unexpected Gift

A number of years ago, the local police officers' association decided that I should be defeated in the upcoming election after I refused to vote for a hefty pay raise for their union members and also declined to support a proposed tax measure to pay for it. They launched a negative campaign to unseat me. The police are generally highly respected in any community, and so their actions represented a dire threat to my re-election.

One of the accusations was that I supported drug dealing in our community because I had championed a "Safe Sleep" program that would allow homeless persons living in their vehicles to legally sleep at night in their vehicles. The program would de-criminalize an innocent activity and reduce discrimination against the homeless population, whose problems were compounded by potential police and public harassment, fines, and court appearances. If they could not pay the fines, their vehicles were subject to impound and warrants were issued for their arrests. The police union claimed that the homeless were notorious drug abusers–often the inherent cause of their homelessness. Thus, I was supporting the local drug trade and even providing a legal place for them to carry out their nefarious activity.

The program I proposed was approved, and effectively limited access to supervised church parking lots where the church congregation voluntarily provided sanitary facilities and on-site management at no public expense. The Salvation Army screened the homeless to weed out those actively using drugs and provided case management. To date, there has been only one call for police assistance to one of these "Safe Sleep" locations—and that was when the homeless folks sleeping in the parking lot observed someone burglarizing the church. I am very proud of this program. It is a good example of how Quaker values can be put into practice for the benefit of the entire community.

A basic fact of political life is that most voters get their information about candidates in ads, mailers, and telephone calls, or in twenty-second sound bites on the local broadcast media. It isn't a world where complex explanations work, and it is expensive to try to respond.

I did not have the resources to reply in kind in the media or otherwise, nor did I have the luxury of time to ponder what to do. But then, by the grace of God, a 'Way' opened. I received a call from a total stranger–someone from another city who had an interest in politics and was fascinated by the barrage of media attacks on me. He said that he had followed my work as a city councilman over the years, and knew that what was happening was so uncharacteristic of what he had seen that it must be an orchestrated smear campaign. He suggested that I provide him with a brief and direct written response to each allegation, saying what was true and what was not, including a statement of why I had done whatever I had done. He told me that he would independently investigate what I provided and, if it proved correct, he would publish that on a website he had created specifically to expose political slander and negative spin.

It could have been a ruse. But I knew instantly that God was was offering me His help. I didn't have to think about it. I simply knew.

I did as the gentleman asked, and he fulfilled his promise. Thereafter, whenever anyone raised one of the allegations, I referred people to that website. In very little time the media stopped printing stories about the allegations, and a groundswell of support rose on my behalf. I won re-election with my highest-ever vote tally.

Social Equity and Democracy

When I was first elected to the City Council, the Mayor asked me what goals and interests I wished to pursue as a member of the Council. I told him that I had an interest in the arts and a commitment to serving our poor and disadvantaged populations. He laughed and replied, "Every Council Member wants to play in the arts with the hoi polloi. You'll be the spear-carrier for the poor and homeless." The Mayor was not being sarcastic. He was reminding me of my lack of seniority on the Council. I have indeed been the "spear-carrier" for the poor and disadvantaged throughout my service to the City, and it has been one of the great sources of satisfaction of my tenure.

Recently in my city, we have been struggling with a controversial program that requires housing developers to provide some low to moderately priced units within each new housing development. In effect this requires the developer, in order to achieve his profit goal, to establish a price structure that offsets the lesser profit of the lower cost unit by charging more for the higher cost unit.

As a matter of public policy, the social benefit of this program is that it assures a minimum supply of affordable housing in what is otherwise a relatively wealthy community. It accommodates a local workforce and reduces traffic. Moreover, it helps create neighborhoods of mixed socioeconomic status. And, it is done at no taxpayer expense, though not without economic and social cost.

Developers argue that the increased price they must seek for the higher-end units has reached a point that inhibits sales, while their critics suggest that all would be well if they only lowered their profit goals. Often neighbors argue that requiring the inclusion of affordable housing within their neighborhoods unfairly and arbitrarily reduces their property values. Underlying this dissension is an ugly element of class struggle and economic discrimination.

I have a great reverence for our form of government. In its genius it seeks to limit the invasion of the rights of the individual by the collective, while at the same time providing a mechanism for assuring civil society the ability to resolve disputes and balance different and competing interests peaceably. Yet, I find it palpably painful to attempt to mediate and resolve these oft-vicious battles over wealth that, in my view, undermine the moral and civic integrity of our community.

These disputes represent the greatest challenge to my ability to bear true witness to my faith. The realpolitik of our world is such that attempting to lead a community while adhering to Quaker precepts and testimonies places one at a distinct disadvantage in a political and economic system designed to accommodate a controlled dog fight over wealth. It is especially challenging when the system places no premium on truth and celebrates the mobilization of combative social and political forces when differences arise.

Though I struggle intensely sometimes when trying to find solutions to public policy issues, I made up my mind many years ago that I would trust in God to lead my heart. So, my struggle is not in weighing this interest against that or figuring out where the political advantage lies. It is in finding and doing the right thing. When I first thought about running for office, I came to the conclusion that if God wanted me to bear the responsibility of public office, I would win election and, if He did not, I would not. I also decided that I would always attempt to be true to the wisdom or insight that He had given me, and never consider the impact of my decisions on my political future. Any defeat at election time was merely God leading me to a different path. One of the greatest satisfactions of my years of service comes from having that assurance.

The Quaker tradition is a curious mélange of inward searching and group validation. One seeks inwardly for God's leading, but given the limitations of one's capacity to interpret that leading, relies on others to confirm it. However, even as this is so, if one is convinced of having a true leading, one must assert it relentlessly, irrespective of differing views expressed by others.

I am often told that I am not sufficiently political because once I have found that leading in my heart, I hang onto it fiercely. Sometimes I am encouraged to curry favor with others in positions of power or to compromise some earnestly-held value in order to better achieve some policy goal. I do build alliances and try to find ways to be helpful to others attempting to achieve their policy goals, so long as I believe they are constructive. But I acknowledge that, once I believe that I have been led to a specific decision or principled stand on a policy matter, I am firm on it. There is no 'standing aside.'

It is difficult to be a leader in such a system of government and be a Quaker. Truth, simplicity, equality and unity are not easily accommodated in our political world, and in effect, inequality and resolution through conflict is a core element of our adversarial system. Nonetheless, when they are evident to the voter, truth and integrity are respected. Commitment to social justice and equality is appreciated, and genuine and persistent attempts to build collaborative and constructive relationships are rewarded with successful public policy serving the entire community. For these reasons I believe it is to Quaker values that I owe much of the modicum of success I have had as a community leader over the years.

A TALE OF THE TALKING STICK:
QUAKER LEADERSHIP
IN THE WIDER CHRISTIAN COMMUNITY

Nancy Thomas

SEVERAL YEARS AGO, I read an article on the Internet posted by
Quaker philosopher, theologian, and poet Arthur Roberts. It was
entitled, "The Talking Stick," and in it Arthur told about crafting a
stick that represents an important Native American tradition, at the
request of a friend who is herself part Cherokee. Since then, he has
fashioned many talking sticks and given them to people who might
use them—elementary teachers, youth workers, and others who lead
group meetings.

I fall under the category of "others," and the article definitely awoke
my interest. From having lived among and studied the traditions of
peoples of other cultures, especially their communication styles, I
understood what Arthur meant when he suggested that the talking
stick might also be called a "listening stick." In many tribal or peasant
cultures, the focus of a communicational event is more on good
listening than on good speaking. Among the Cherokees, the chief
passes the talking stick to whoever has the right to speak, and the rest
of the group assumes the concurrent right to listen carefully. It's more
than a matter of taking turns; it involves a shared responsibility and
is the Cherokee manner of "doing all things decently and in order."

In a letter that accompanied the article, Arthur invited any of us who
would like a talking stick, to approach him. I thought of the class I was

scheduled to teach and decided to experiment. Arthur let me choose from his collection, and I picked a branch with some artistic twists and knots, beautifully finished with skillful craftsmanship. I put it in my suitcase, and in August of that year my husband Hal and I traveled to Asuncion, Paraguay for two weeks of seminars, including my one-week intensive on "Culture, Spirituality and Mission."

I intended to use the stick symbolically, in part to represent the spirituality of a particular tribal culture, and in part to encourage the class to listen well to each other. I did not imagine a literal use, to aid in taking turns, feeling that more appropriate for young people. These seminars were part of a doctoral program in theology, and the ten students in my class were all leaders in their denominations; several pastored churches with over 1,000 members. They came from Argentina, Brazil, Chile, Ecuador, Guatemala, Puerto Rico, Mexico, Hispanic Canada, and the USA; and they represented groups as diverse as Presbyterians, Baptists, Nazarenes and Pentecostals. And here I was, a Quaker woman in the middle of everything, trying to bring it all together.

I began the class Monday morning with a devotional, using the talking stick, describing Cherokee customs and the importance of good listening. I then reminded the class of Jesus, the Teacher in our midst. I symbolically gave the talking stick to Jesus and placed it on the table in the center of this circle of scholars and learners, among whom I felt privileged (and a little frightened) to be a member. And that was that.

Or so I thought.

Near the end of the week, on Thursday morning, we were discussing the shadow side of spirituality, wrestling with sin, Satan, and the problem of evil. Coming from diverse cultural and theological backgrounds, each student brought to the table a distinct perspective. Sometimes the discussions in these classes get loud and lively. This was one of those times. At one point, about five people were speaking at once, and the decibel level was rising. Of a quiet nature myself, I usually shy away from these types of encounters. Unless, of course, I'm in the role of teacher, and then I struggle to find a helpful way through. Having a soft voice does not help.

But at the precise moment I needed it, inspiration struck. I stood up, in the middle of the noise and confusion, walked to the table in the center and held up the talking stick. The room exploded into silence.

Confusion registered on the faces of some. Others seemed a bit affronted. ("What's this crazy woman trying to do?") But slowly light began to dawn. Without a word I walked over and handed the stick to Jorge, a usually quiet-spoken man whose observations had set off this controversy. It was still 'his turn.' He took the stick, paused a moment, then held it high in the air, a grin of victory on his face. Everyone laughed and seemed relieved. I still wasn't sure how this would turn out. After all, these were not elementary school students.

The next forty-five minutes were fascinating. The students themselves negotiated the passing of the talking stick, and took it most seriously, at the same time accepting a certain playfulness in the practice. The discussion continued on the same level of passion and intentionality, but with what I discerned as a new level of listening. More than trading points of view, a spirit of responsiveness to each other became evident. There was obvious relief in the sense of order, facilitated by the talking stick. By the end of the morning, while we still hadn't definitively solved the problem of evil, we had clarified some of the important questions and received insight. Class consensus was that it had been a significant and enlightening discussion. Not to mention fun.

I didn't expect to use the stick again, but the next day, the last day of the class, in the middle of another heated discussion, one of the students went over and picked up the talking stick. Again, laughter. And again, a willingness to let an instrument facilitate order, an order that did not stifle, but rather channeled communication.

At the end of the day, and of the class, Jorge came up to thank me, and I had another inspiration. I had previously decided that if the talking stick proved meaningful to the class, even if only symbolically, I would give it away to one of the students. I acknowledged Jorge's gratitude and handed him the stick, asking if he would like to take it home to Ecuador with him. He asked with surprise, "You want to give this to me?" I assured him that was indeed the case, and his smile as he took it from my hands still warms me.

It interests me to know that one of the reasons the dean of this multidenominational school invited me to teach the class on spirituality was because I am Quaker. He is convinced that the lively, largely extroverted Latin American Protestant movement needs exposure to Quaker values.

What aspects of Quaker leadership values does the talking-stick experience illustrate? The conviction that Christ, the light of God, somehow illumines every person speaks to the temptation of the leader to consider herself the "expert" (nasty little word). We are aware that the task of the teacher is to encourage active participation in the adventure of learning, so that everyone might draw from and share their own experience, knowledge and insight. While this may not be a particularly Quaker insight, our focus on the universal light of Christ encourages a more horizontal leadership style, especially in the teaching role.

The belief that the light of Christ somehow illumines cultures as well as people let me respectfully draw from the Cherokee culture in a theological class on Christian spirituality. It made a difference.

The sense of "Jesus as the Presence in our midst" powerfully affects my leadership style, giving me courage, perspective and the hope that something real and good will result from a particular gathering. I even used the famous Quaker painting of that name by J. Doyle Penrose in my introductory PowerPoint presentation to this class. I let the talking stick symbolize the fact that Jesus is our Teacher. To me, this isn't wishy-washy mystical spirituality; it's reality, and it affects how I teach and how I respond to those in my class. We are all disciples of Jesus, and Jesus is actually with us.

Other Quaker values that came out in the class include the focus on good listening and the bent toward non-violence. I love a lively discussion, but if there comes a point when emotions and egotism get out of hand, we need a calming influence, a means to slow down and find our way back to respect and listening. As a teacher, I don't always do this well, but I'm learning.

As a leader and a teacher, I'm grateful that I walk with Jesus. And it's good to realize that in every situation where I am called to play a leading role, Christ is somehow in every other person in the gathering, our Teacher, our Guide, our Leader.

LOSS OF FAITH

Eleanor Dart

H OW DO WE recognize a leading? When I first applied to work as
a civilian counselor on U.S. military installations, I didn't know
that I was being led. I simply felt, when I heard about the program,
"Oh, yes, I've got to do that." I felt it clearly enough to persist through
six months of applications, interviews, security checks, and training,
until I landed at an Army base in Germany in June of 2006, having
had exactly *no* prior experience of any kind with the military.

Very soon, as I encountered the difficulties and suffering of military
personnel and their families, those so often unidentified victims of
our ongoing wars, I knew myself to be doing peace work for which I
was exactly suited. I felt completely engaged, heart and soul, and I was
immensely grateful. I believe this joyful gratitude, even in the midst
of grief and pain, is one sign that a leading is true.

Between overseas assignments, I brought my clearness to Pima
Meeting, and asked the meeting to consider releasing me to do this
work, since the demands of the work left me no energy or time
to devote to the ongoing needs of my Meeting. At that time most
Friends were familiar with providing support to conscientious
objectors, to veterans, and to AWOL soldiers, but not to active-duty
military. This has now changed, as evident in the "On War" January/
February 2013 edition of *Western Friend*. But in 2006, Pima Meeting

was not in unity to identify me as a released Friend, as one who is acting for the meeting. Some Friends felt that my work was an indirect way of supporting the U.S. war machine. Others felt I was indeed acting for them, and offered long-distance listening and much loving help to me during the next five years. I believe that the discussion my request inspired was of value to Pima Friends.

As a counselor, and as a person who is open to the guidance of the Spirit, I listen, not so much to an internal "still, small voice," but to my body. There seems to be a sort of magnetic wisdom in the region of my heart, which vibrates and informs me. The story below is one example of my following such a leading. I have changed details so as not to identify the person involved.

Loss of Faith

Soon after I arrived on this U.S. Army base in Italy, I was introduced to one of the chaplains, a Catholic priest originally from Puerto Rico, but most recently living in a monastic community in the States. He had not volunteered to join the military, but was ordered by his Bishop to serve for four years, as a number of priests are now asked to do. He is a young man, slight of build and soft-spoken. In the dining facility on the day we met, he briefly mentioned that he had spent a year in Iraq, and that it had been very hard for him. He didn't say more, but I sensed his profound distress.

It seemed to me that this was a man who needed help, but was unlikely to ask for it. I went to visit him in the Chaplain's Office on base.

We talked briefly about his work. He spoke in heavily accented English, and told me that many on base either can't understand him, or don't take the trouble to try. He asked me why I had come to see him. I said that I had felt led to come, that it seemed to me that he was in trouble. I gently invited him to talk, and he opened his heart to me.

For twelve months this quiet soul was the only priest available to soldiers in one half of the theater of war. He was constantly on the move, constantly under fire, literally running from armored vehicle to helicopter and down onto his knees in the dust and dirt beside dying soldiers, every single day. He tried to show up to offer mass, confession, and last rites to any soldier who wanted a priest.

He was completely alone. Never in one place long enough to make a friend. Not attached to any unit. No one to talk to, in part because he is a priest, and as such is perceived to have God's support and not to need ordinary human help. In that crazy place during those months, there was no one who was concerned about him, no one who had time to even notice. After all, everyone there is under fire. Perhaps you can imagine. Perhaps not.

Since his return, no one had asked him about his experiences in the active theater of war, and he had not talked to anyone about them. That day he talked to me.

He spoke about how angry he has been since coming back from Iraq. "I've never been angry like this before," he said. "But this just took over, filled me. I would be angry at people I didn't know, in check-out lines at the store, in traffic. I'd say so; I'd act on it; I'd yell and shake my fist. I was so angry at some unkind people at work I would think about ways to hurt them." He was afraid he might have to break the vow he made to his bishop, and get out of the army in order not to actually hurt someone. But he knew it wouldn't help, he'd still be angry, even then. He told me he was using journaling and prayer to intervene on his irrational fury, and that, slowly, it was helping.

Finally he told me the worst thing he had experienced downrange, of inhaling the roasted meat smell of a burned soldier. Running as fast as he could to give last rites, hoping to reach the soldier before death, out of breath, he pushed through a crowd of doctors. "And I am a small man, so my face was right there by what had been his face, and I breathed him in, deep breaths because I had been running. When I went to the dining place after that I would smell the meat cooking, and I couldn't eat. I only ate cookies for a week. Just cookies."

"I am wrong now, all wrong. I can't sleep or rest. I can't eat. I am angry; I feel hatred. I feel that I have lost my faith."

We spoke together for a long time. We talked about physiology, about the normal response of the nervous system when humans witness violent death. We spoke about post-traumatic stress and the effects of mild concussion—he had been close enough to one IED explosion that he lost his hearing for ten minutes. I helped him understand that his anger and isolation are results of the trauma of war, of that great tragedy. I described treatment that could be available to him. He said he hadn't thought that these things, which he knew about, might apply to him. He had believed that faith alone should protect him, and that his suffering meant a loss of faith.

I imagine that what he told me that day was just a small part of the memories and visions he carries, but it contained the essence. I watched his spirit lighten, watched his laughter return. Told him that the gift of being wounded is to heal oneself, and be better able ever after to help the wounded. A painful gift. I spoke of the blessing he has been to others, and will be. He said to know that someone, anyone, cared enough to listen and understand, was redemptive for him.

When I left he put his hand on his heart, and thanked me. A dear sweet man. I am so very grateful that I was given this gift, called to be present, listen and offer comfort. This is what I was there to do. And I got to do it. *Deus Gracias*. My heart is full.

BETWEEN REALITY AND POSSIBILITY: LEADING INTO THE GAP

C. Wess Daniels

ONE OF THE GREAT IRONIES of the religious movement known as "Friends" is that you don't have to look very far to find tension and conflict. One of the questions that currently baffles me most isn't where the tension comes from or what we should do about it, but how do we build communities that allow for the tension created by our differences to be transformative and heart-opening? How can we make our faith communities into spaces where we foster empathy for one another and see within each other the possibilities presented through God's grace working in our lives?

Recently, I had the chance to go to Philadelphia to participate in a consultation with a Quaker foundation. Fifteen young Friends from different branches of Quakerism were invited to be a part of the foundation's discernment about the future of their investments. The thought was to turn to Friends' young leaders in hopes of gleaning useful ideas about where the Religious Society of Friends is headed in the next twenty-five years. I have no idea if the board members got what they hoped for, but I thought the meeting was inspiring! Here, gathered together at Friends Center in downtown Philly, were fifteen bright, energized, and creative young Quaker leaders. All were doing their best to be faithful to their own leadings, hailing from varied backgrounds and places along the Quaker spectrum.

The old joke goes that if you get more than one Quaker in the room there is bound to be a disagreement, especially on religious matters, and in a room of fifteen young Friends you might expect to find fifteen different understandings of God, faith, and Quakerism. Yet from the moment I arrived, I had a very distinct sense of being in a safe space and welcomed by community. There was a tension these Friends were able to embrace that made the space both affirming and lively, filled with honesty and grace. I think some of this simply had to do with our not being invested in perpetuating the family dysfunction, and I have no doubt if we had enough time together we would have at least more clearly identified our differences. But the sense of instant connection and inclusion was what stood out to me.

During the gathering, one of the groups sharing ideas put its finger on a primary tension that all of our meetings, yearly meetings, and tradition knows too well. They said: "Quakerism is open to all people, but it isn't whatever you want it to be." As they wrote these words on the whiteboard, silent agreement appeared around the room.

Here are two questions for you, the reader: What is the tension being held here? And what do you hear when you read that statement?

I gather that it could mean that while we are open to all, no one individual has the power to decide or control the direction of the group. Holding the tension of community together takes a process of listening and coming to clearness before God before we move on anything. Many of us believe that only Jesus, who is living and present, gets to be our Teacher, final Word, and guiding Light. So, while Quakerism is an "open-source" movement, as my friend Peggy Parsons likes to say, it is not whatever you or I want it to be. It is open, but it is subject to the direction of God within the gathered community, guided by our collective knowledge.

Inclusion, Possibility, and Leading in the Tragic Gap

Not only is it true that our faith communities are filled with tensions, but so is the rest of life. Some of the tensions we find are in our relationships, jobs, families, aging, health, and social injustices. In all of these tensions we are faced with what Parker Palmer calls the tragic gap between reality and new possibility. In our lives we experience a divide between the reality we live in and the hope that we aspire to, between heaven and earth, between realism and idealism. There is often a difference, for me at least, between where the GPS says I am and where I meant to be and this 'gap' creates tension in all of us. So we gravitate to one pole or the other: pulverising realism or impervious idealism. But, rather than resolve this tension by moving to one pole or the other, as leaders we are called to "stand in the tragic gap." We are invited to hold the tension and lead in the midst of the tragic gap.

In other words, to be truly open means to include the dissenting voices, the doubters, the "minority" positions, and the betrayers. This was the practice of Jesus' "table fellowship" throughout the gospels. Back then, who ate with whom was essential. It was partly about being righteous religiously, but it was also about social class. In the time of Jesus, who you ate with was a statement about who you saw as equals. So when Jesus dines with fishermen, tax collectors, sex workers, Roman soldiers, zealots, people with disabilities, drunkards, Pharisees, you name it, he was breaking all kinds of rules. If you've watched any British TV at all you know that the chauffeur is not supposed to sit down and eat with the lord of the manor! Or As Ryan Bolger likes to say, "The problem with Jesus isn't that he ate with people, it's who he ate with. Jesus invited all the 'wrong' people to be his dinner guests."

Consider those Jesus included at his final meal. It's a beautiful and challenging picture of his ability to hold the tension in his community. In Luke 22:14-34, the author refers not only to Jesus' betrayer being one of the people invited over for dinner, but also to Peter's betrayal, and to the disciples who totally miss the point about his death and are more concerned about who was to be Jesus' successor. Luke's gospel foreshadows these betrayals and yet Jesus still ate with them as equals. Jesus' supper table is an act that projects what is possible within the "kingdom of God" right here, right now.

Another example of this tension of the tragic gap between reality and possibility has to do with my five year-old daughter and her severe food allergies. She is allergic to peanuts, almonds, eggs, gluten, dairy, citrus and probably other things we've yet to identity. When we finally diagnosed her allergies, we felt both a huge sense of relief and bewilderment. Now we knew how to help her desert-dry itchy skin, but we also had to go through a major lifestyle transition. And of course, all of her favorite foods were not on the new list of foods she could eat.

Today she often finds herself at school, friends' houses, community gatherings and birthday parties where she is unable to eat most of the 'fun' foods her friends are eating. She has learned at a very young age what it feels like to be left out. One of the ways she has coped with this is through imaginative play with her three-year-old sister. Their favorite game is "Family," and everyone in the game has food allergies. Part of the game is where she tells her imaginative playmates, or her sister, "You can't eat that because you are allergic, but you can eat this..."

At first I thought this was a strange thing to play, but then it dawned on me: in her imaginative play everyone has allergies and therefore she is no longer left out. Furthermore, because everyone has allergies, everyone knows how it feels and thus can empathize with her. If I were her I would have pretended to eat bowl after bowl of ice-cream and pizza! But instead of pretending there is a magical cure, she creates a world with an enriched level of empathy and everyone is equalized by a shared point of view. Her reality is one in which people don't understand just how difficult it is to be five years old and have terrible allergies and eczema, and what it feels like to be left out of so much of the fun. Thus, in her play world of new possibility, no one is left out.

The work of Quaker leadership is being able to experience the tensions found within our communities as transformative possibilities and stand within the tragic gap of reality and possibility in a way that 'breaks the rules of acceptability' and builds on fostering better empathy with others. In my view, the best leadership finds ways to hold the tension between reality and possibility, while working to expand the perspectives and capacity for empathy within a community.

Expanding Umwelt, Expanding Empathy

In her book, *Journey Inward Journey Outward*, Elizabeth O'Connor writes about Esther Harding, a biologist who argued that all of nature has a very limited awareness of the inward and outward world. In her studies she found that every creature, both great and small, only sees and hears what concerns itself—it ignores everything else. Following this, Harding suggests that each animal lives in a world of its own or *Umwelt*, a German word that means "environment" but can be translated as "self-centered world." Every creature has its own Umwelt to which it responds while ignoring everything else.

To illustrate, Harding gives the example of the wood tick. A wood tick needs blood from a warm-blooded animal in order to reproduce. When the time has come it attaches itself to a tree, sticks its thumb out, and waits to hitch a ride on an unsuspecting mammal passerby. Because there are so many wood ticks in the forest and not enough warm-blooded animals to go around, Harding says that some wood ticks have waited for a ride for as long as 17 years! The wood tick is so fixed on its own situation that it will not change trees, move around, or find an alternative. A wood tick is an animal unable to hold the tension between reality and possibility. It is unable to expand its horizons to change in a way that could make its life better.

We can be caught in this kind of limited Umwelt too. Many times we find ourselves in need of making adjustments, changing our expectations, or learning how to do something new—and yet we will just hang on that same darn tree for 17 years, refusing to budge. It is easy to be like the wood tick and only focus on what concerns us, to live in a self-centered world, while being blind to the realities of others. The Quaker leader helps the worshipping community to move out into the world, out into challenges and transforming experiences so that it won't be caught on the same tree 17 years later, starved and alone.

Do Not Remember the Former Things

The broader our Umwelts, the easier it is for us to be able to hold the tensions of reality and possibility, and the more capable we become of growing and moving past those stuck places in our spiritual and emotional lives. The hard part is that having our Umwelts expanded can make us feel fragile. Just the thought of having our lives changed in some significant way causes a lot of fear and anxiety. We are afraid our hearts will break.

I see it kind of like breaking in a baseball glove. When my dad helped me break in my first glove we put oil on it repeatedly, stuck a ball in the pocket of the mitt and then held the glove closed around the ball with a couple of rubber bands. Then we let it sit for what felt like years. The goal was to make it more pliable, easier to open and close quickly, with a pre-formed indentation where the baseball would magically fall. It never did that last part for me, but you see the point. Can we move from having brittle to pliable hearts? Maybe our hearts need to be broken in like the baseball glove.

As our hearts become more pliable, the more readily we are able to accept the differences of those around us and the new possibilities that break upon us by God's grace. We might define grace as God's help expanding each of our Umwelts of our hearts and imaginations. I believe that this is the kind of work that Jesus was constantly engaged in, as were Paul, John of Patmos, and the Hebrew Prophets.

Consider the passage found in Isaiah 43:16-21, which was written most likely in the late sixth century during the Hebrew exile in Babylon. There was a lot of suffering in this time, and people felt the weight of oppression from their Babylonian captors. The hearers of the prophetic message are invited to have their Umwelts expanded so that they can be ready for the new thing that God is about to do.

The first part of this text reminds the people of their foundational liberation narrative of the Exodus. The God who hears their concerns now is the same God who has worked to liberate them in the past, who "makes a way in the sea, a path in the mighty waters." Babylon is no match for YHWH. When times are difficult, when the tensions get to be too much, we are to first move back and draw on our collective memory of the ways in which God has helped us, brought us life, and walked us through the valley of death.

But then the text says something even more interesting. "Do not remember the former things, or consider the things of old. I am about to do a new thing: now it springs forth, do you not perceive it?"

In other words, the wood tick is called to get down out of the tree. The baseball mitt is prepped for oiling. The hands slowly turn upwards, opening from clenched fists to a friendly, receptive position. God is about to do something different, unexpected, and the people are challenged by the prophet to be prepared to receive it.

I do not think the prophet is suggesting we throw out our tradition, and become purely individualistic persons cut free from the narrative of community. That would be to repeat the sins of modernity. What I think the author is saying by placing these two poles of reality and possibility next to one another is that it is important to embrace your tradition and story, without being limited by it. Do not let it become the excuse for clinging to a limited Umwelt. Instead, be ready to have your imaginations broken open by the Living God. If you are the wood tick and every time up until now, hanging out on this old tree really worked for you, it may be time for a new way. The prophet-as-leader is the one who reminds the community of their shared story, while also helping the people to forget "the former things" so they are able to traverse new contexts, meet new challenges, or respond in faithfulness to fresh calls that God may be leading them into.

Up until a few months ago, I was spinning my wheels with my dissertation. I had done all my research. I had even written four or five chapters, yet if a person asked what it was about, they would fall comatose before I could finish explaining the project. Each new question about the project became a new opportunity for me to try to figure out what I was doing. I had all the pieces and parts, but I kept running into the same brick wall. It seemed I was just hanging on that tree, waiting year after year for a deer to walk by.

Then one afternoon while I was sitting in my favorite coffeeshop, it hit me. I had a notebook sitting open, and the pages were filled with summaries of everything I had been working on. But a blank page stared up at me. I felt like I had a cart full of treasure but I couldn't convince anyone that what I had found was worth a dime. What I began to tell myself was to forget how I had understood it in the past. Then, as I gazed out the sun-filled window, I fell into a kind of daydream. I don't know how long I sat there or how it happened, but eventually and out of nowhere a number of images came to me that synthesized and summarized my entire project in ways I had never considered before. Every piece of the puzzle fell into place for me, and it finally made sense. Finally, in an off-hand moment, at the breaking point of frustration, I let go of what I knew and something new came.

The old methods, all the summaries, all the ways I had tried to bring my project together failed. I didn't have to throw out my research, but I had to let go of it just long enough that it could be reassembled in a new way, with new insights and possibilities. It was in that moment that the rest of my dissertation wrote itself. Every chapter fell into place and everything made sense in a way I could never have planned or manufactured. Now I can even explain what my project is over Twitter: I have developed a model of renewal for faith traditions that is both convergent and participatory.

"Do not Remember..." is the prophet's way of saying don't get stuck waxing nostalgic about the 'good old days.' Don't just expect that repeating the same things over and over again will make everything okay. Callie Plunket-Brewton says:

> The prophet aims to create an imaginative space in the minds of the people so that their conception of the past can transform their

understanding of the present and, thus, the future: "I am about to do a new thing; now it springs forth, do you not perceive it?" In a seemingly hopeless situation, the prophet calls on the people not to lose heart but to look with anticipation for the signs of God's approaching redemption, for the "new thing" that is coming.

Silence can help to create that imaginative space. Scripture can expand our imaginations. Gazing off into space in a daydream can be met by a still small voice. But waxing nostalgic will not aid us in leadership; it will not help us to hold the tensions that exist in our own inner-lives or in our meetings. We may refuse change and use God as our excuse, but could it be that God is the one who is initiating the change in our communities?

Until the Words Fall In

I love that Isaiah 43 in the Bible names the tensions between reality and the possibility of something new that God is about to do with his people and invites us to imagine what could be. It is meant to be a surprise, a kind of shattering of what we expect so that the hearers might have a new capacity to hear something new. It is like a favorite story of mine that Parker Palmer shares in *A Hidden Wholeness*:

> There is an old Hasidic tale that tells us how such things happen. The pupil comes to the rebbe and asks, "Why does the Torah tell us to 'place these words upon your hearts?' Why does it not tell us to place these holy words *in* our hearts?" The rebbe answers, "It is because as we are, our hearts are closed, and we cannot place the holy words in our hearts. So we place them on top of our hearts. And there they stay until, one day, the heart breaks, and the words fall in."

We are often afraid to enter into the difficult space between holding tensions and allowing our imaginations to be opened up, for fear our hearts will be broken. It is very possible that we will discover we have been wrong about something. We may find that others have legitimate and deeply held beliefs and experiences that are different from our own. We may hear stories that are too painful to bear, or find ourselves powerless in the face of tragedy over which we have no power. It is always possible that entering a difficult space while seeking to hold tensions may result in experiencing a loss, but if it is grounded by God's grace, then that brokenness can bring us into a new ability to love, listen, and empathize with one another.

When was the last time your heart was broken open like this?

A couple years ago, our oldest daughter was getting ready for bed and she asked me, her resident theologian, "Daddy, why did God give me allergies?" The wind was knocked out of me. What a heartbreaking and direct question. I did my best to take it in stride. I said, "Well, honey," (I was already losing steam) "God didn't give those allergies to you. Sometimes things like this just happen."

Good job, Mr. No-Emotion. She looked blankly at me. It was clear that answer didn't help her at all. She fell silent. I took what seemed like a second chance and tried again. I said, "What I mean to say is, I don't know why you have allergies, but it makes me very angry that you do. I wish you didn't have them and you didn't have to go through this. Mommy and I will do our very best to help you through this." Not only was that the better answer for her, it was the right answer.

I moved from defending God to defending my little girl. This is my role as Daddy, just as my role as shepherd of a spiritual community is to be on the side of those in my care. I moved from trying to avoid her pain to accepting it and allowing it to hit me squarely. In doing so I was broken open, but it enabled me to help her carry it.

I am convinced that this is in keeping with a God who also sides with the victims throughout human history as scripture so clearly illustrates. When we are afraid to be hurt or experience loss, we will find ourselves defending God, holding others' pain at a distance, and trying to resolve the tensions that exist within ourselves and our communities. But if we allow ourselves to take the hit squarely and be broken open, I think we will gain a new capacity to love and have empathy for those in our care.

I believe that it is not only possible, but *desirable*, to be broken into a new capacity. Just as the Hebrew people would come to desire that new thing God would do in their midst—even if it meant leaning into the difficult unknowns of wilderness life—they would receive that gift.

It is possible to live with a greater capacity for acceptance and love, but it will not be easy and our hearts may be broken in the process. My prayer is that our hearts are not shattered, but broken open into that new capacity.

As we grow into deeper relationship with those whose values and experiences are different from ours, with those whose pain is deep and whose true selves have been barred access by the gatekeepers of religion and society, the horizons of our little worlds are pushed back, our Umwelts are enlarged and our hearts are broken open. Quaker leadership needs now more than ever people who are able to graciously hold these tensions and to set a table for everyone who wants to come and eat. If it is true that "Quakerism is open to all people, but it isn't whatever you [or I] want it to be," then we must guide our communities in a direction that will be able to hold this tension even if the way is yet unmarked.

Acting

Laura Magnani
Peggy Parsons
Diane Randall
Stephen McNeil
Bill and Genie Durland

IF LISTENING IS THE HEART of faith for Friends, then discernment is the practice that breaks open that heart to the world, letting in compassion. The actions that spring from people who have engaged in discernment and are grounded and clear in their motives—those who exhibit an inner strength—can be incredibly effective and powerful. They may also be unexpected, or not look very much at all like an action or a response to the casual observer.

Years ago, a friend of mine who was also a Quaker fell gravely ill, and was admitted to the hospital. For days she faded in and out of consciousness, and we feared she would not survive. As she was moved from floor to floor, a simple postcard-sized card followed her, landing each time on her bedside table. In plain black typeface, it read, "I am a Quaker. In case of an emergency, please be quiet."

I believe the humorous wisdom of that card is one of the things that ultimately kept her alive. It's also a wonderful illustration of how very different "action" may look when it's undertaken by a Quaker. Make no mistake: There is a long tradition among Friends of taking very public, very controversial stands that even today may land them in prison. Equally common are thsoe whose actions are subtle and unseen. Both follows paths which first lead through listening for divine, inner guidance, then to discernment within one's self and with others to clarify that yes, the direction is fully understood: this is what we are led to do. And *then* comes the action.

The essays in this section range widely in their examples of acting. There are themes of both quiet witness and of direct, public action. In each one, you will see evidence of that inner strength the Nobel Committee marveled at in 1947. And if the new faces that appeared in my meeting during the Occupy! protests—pulled in by the way in which Friends were present in their community—are evidence of anything at all, it is that there is a palpable hunger in the world for such energy. Our example—imperfect though it is—is greatly needed.

Queries on Acting

Several of the pieces in this section show Friends taking action in ways that might seem unusual, or even to work against succeeding in their goals. Do you understand why they did what they did? Which of these stories speaks to you most, and why?

Laura points out that "Servanthood is not just a role reserved for clerks." What do you feel she means by that? When you are not in a leadership role, how do you contribute to the community's discernment to act?

Do you agree with Diane's assertion that citizenship is a form of leadership? Why or why not?

Share a story you find inspiring of an individual or group engaging in careful, grounded, and Spirit-led action. What is meaningful to you about this story or experience?

SERVANT LEADERSHIP
INSIDE AND OUTSIDE THE FOLD

Laura Magnani

H OW FRIENDS do leadership is one of the best-kept secrets around.
It is not the kind of secret that is whispered behind backs or the
kind (of which there are many in the Quaker tradition) that certain
important people just know about and enforce. Rather it is the great
set of processes that say no one will hold a job more than a few years,
positions will be rotated, and most will find themselves serving in
a variety of capacities over decades. I can't vouch for this being the
culture of Quakers throughout the country, but among Western
Friends it has represented the genius of our system.

The most common expression for this type of leadership is "servant
leadership." One example of how it manifests internally is with the
concept of the "clerk," a term that announces the sense in which the
presiding Friend guiding a meeting serves the community as a leader
in a non-traditional sense. Yet, of course the deeper demonstration of
servant leadership is really about discipleship, the extent to which we
are able to be servants to God's leadings. It is a humiliating process—a
process of humbling oneself, rather than some kind of exultation or
elevation. And the test of such servanthood is not what the clerk does
or doesn't do, but whether the community discerns that God's purposes
have been served by the actions taken—not whether one side won over
another, or whether stronger arguments were made by one faction.

So we may be talking more about the absence of leadership, partly manifested by the extent to which we have eschewed hierarchy–refusing to give more power to some, or to defer to those "at the top" to set policies or determine decisions.

What can such non-leaders do, when serving the community?

1. *Set the agenda.* Some might say this is a huge amount of power – until you realize that whatever is set can be unset by the gathered body, and likely will be.

2. *Set a tone.* This is no small matter, especially if it succeeds in grounding the group and keeping worship at the center.

3. *Gather the sense of the Meeting*, except when it is revised, restated, or not approved by the body.

There are definite dangers in such a community concept of leadership – particularly if individuals see themselves as having a veto power over the body as a whole, or even simply as a platform for any view they may have. It is relatively easy to hijack the process, partly because of such understated "leadership." It puts a crucial responsibility on each of us to hold this process as sacred and to also see ourselves as servants. Servanthood is not just a role reserved for clerks.

Friends in the World

But how is the Friends' concept of leadership played out in our work beyond the internal—our work in the world? Certainly the myriad of Friends' organizations, focusing on issues of importance to us, is a way of exerting leadership in the world. We have seen this in social justice issues, within our work in education, within the many Friends' agencies that serve people in the last stages of their lives. We have led by example, by creating the kinds of institutions that operate according to the principles we hold dear.

In the case of the American Friends Service Committee (AFSC), Friends Committee on National Legislation (FCNL), and Friends Committee on Legislation- California (FCLCA), we have advocated for positions in the wider world, that we think Spirit would call us to—what I might call Gospel Order, but others might just consider "social justice for all." Within those organizations are individuals with exemplary qualities—many we'd call leaders—some even heroes. They have been both Friends and non-Friends.

I have always felt that the person I learned the most from about representing Friends values was my mentor at the Friends Committee on Legislation- California (FCLCA), Joe Gunterman. He was the lobbyist for the organization for 14 years, between 1962 and 1976, and we worked together for the last four of those years. He is not a Friend, or a member of any faith group. He was a conscientious objector in World War II, which put him in touch with a lot of Friends, as well as Jehovah's Witnesses, Mennonites, Brethren and other radicals. For its sixty-year history, the FCLCA has only had Friends in the lobbyist position less than half the time, although Friends have been well represented through the committee process. And Friends have also been represented by our non-Quaker representatives.

Before saying more about Joe, it should be observed that this absence of Quaker lobbyists says something about leadership all by itself. If our witness is strong and clear, likeminded people will find us and will take up our cause. We never thought we had a corner on the market on truth or right thinking or just causes. We are a small group, numbering for decades now only about 1,500 liberal, unprogrammed Friends in all of California. Groups like the FCLCA would have died out long ago if Quakers were the sole source of staff, volunteers, and donors.

My initial introduction to Quaker leadership began, like so many things, as an accident. In 1969 a professor of mine at UC Berkeley suggested that a friend and I go up to Sacramento and see how the Legislature was responding to the riots happening on college campuses. We were sophomores, newly minted practitioners of non-violence, not looking for a "fight" (or a non-fight, one might say), as much as an opportunity to see what our persuasive powers could do. Though not averse to protest, campus demonstrations in the heart of the Free Speech Movement sometimes degenerated into rock-throwing and name-calling. This professor had worked with Joe Gunterman on fair housing legislation and knew the FCLCA was a multi-issue organization that would be concerned about the plight of students and the public education system.

Being carless, and generally speaking penniless, we hitchhiked to Sacramento for our 11:00 a.m. appointment. Joe briefed us on how the campus situation was perceived by lawmakers and showed us the stack of bills—approximately 100 of them—meant to crack down on students. Everything was in that pile, from withdrawing financial aid from students who demonstrated to building a fence around the

University to exclude "outside agitators." We needed to show these legislators the human face of students, he emphasized—not the ones they were seeing in the newspapers. It is significant that he did not try to convince us what we should say, or what the FCLCA would say-but simply how the process worked, and how our gifts as students could have an impact.

As I look back on it now, this encounter can only be seen as a "wooing process." As we sat waiting to discuss strategy with a sympathetic senator, Joe's wife, Emmy, scurried by the office, spotted us, and suggested Joe bring us home for lunch. Their children were home putting soup and homemade bread on the table. We gladly accepted, but first we had our first meeting with a legislator.

In a way it wasn't fair. Senator Dunlap was far from typical—he even had kids of his own at other UC campuses. But he and Joe walked us through the do's and don'ts of "cause lobbying" and watched closely to see how we approached the conversation. Would we try to find common ground, or would we lead with our 19-year-old righteousness? How well could we articulate the issues facing students? How would we respond when faced with outright disagreement? Senator Dunlap was quiet, thoughtful, and encouraging. We left feeling like we had a contribution to make. In the afternoon we met with one of the legislative leaders—a committee or caucus chair. Again, the focus was on advice and possible strategies.

Before letting us go that afternoon, Joe asked us to come back the following week, with as many students as we could find who were directly involved with the demonstrations. If we succeeded, Joe promised a crash course in lobbying, as well as appointments with a broad cross-section of legislators.

Whether it was divine intervention, hard work, or sheer luck, we carpooled back to Sacramento with about a dozen students involved in the struggle to establish a Third World College on campus, hoping the needs of students of color would be more realistically addressed both academically and socially. We didn't look much like ourselves—dressed mostly in suits and ties and dresses—and we squeezed into the tiny FCLCA office for our half-hour orientation to "cause lobbying," the kind where your only tool is reliable information.

We paired off, men and women, and managed to see 17 legislators in one day! We were hooked. Legislators didn't expect to find so many college students so easy to talk to. They didn't expect a Third

World College to be anything other than a communist plot. Today the College of Ethnic Studies at UC Berkeley awards PhD's and is fully integrated into the university system. Chances are, those legislators had no idea what role the FCLCA played in these encounters.

Joe was practicing a form of servant leadership that enabled an educational process to unfold—ours and the legislators. It did, in fact, further the issues of the FCLCA in the areas of education and racial equality, but not with the goal of winning points for the organization. Instead it was to put a human face on a demonized group—in this case students. In the interest of fairness, it is important to add that if we had walked into the FCLCA office hoping to put a gun in the hands of every man, woman, and child in the state, he probably would not have been so accommodating. He might have spent time trying to re-direct our energies, he might have given us the address of a more "like-minded group," or he might have pleaded ignorance.

What Joe emanated in the day-to-day workings of his job was a quiet, very grounded, ideologically pure form of nonviolent action. Guided by policy statements which articulated broad principles, he was free to determine Friends' perspectives on many issues. There wasn't an instance, in my years working with him, when his reading of the policies was questioned.

Joe has always been a master of understatement—incarnating a version of Friends' leadership that refused to exaggerate, stuck scrupulously to the facts, and rarely took credit for victories. Joe, probably to a fault, never used the pronoun "I" when he wrote stories for the FCLCA monthly newsletter. They were always about the issues or about the organization. Some might say this editorial style carried Friends' reluctance to evangelize to an extreme. After all, lobbyists are supposed to pressure lawmakers, to convince them of their way of thinking, to win them over. But the pressure he was exerting had more to do with creating an environment where they wanted to do the right thing—where they dared to take a moral stance even when it was not politically advantageous.

That is harder and harder to do these days. Term limits (under which lawmakers are constantly vying for the next office they will seek), complex issues, and vast amounts of special interest money all interfere. It is also harder in an era of branding, self promotion, and competition among cause lobbyists. Taking a pure stand in a legislative arena is virtually impossible.

Among the legislative directors who followed Joe, both Quaker and non-Quakers, few would claim to be in the same league with Joe. His underlying philosophy never varied. He would say, "Quakers believe in that of God in everyone. That applies to housing, to jobs, to education, to basic human dignity for every person, regardless of their circumstance or even of the actions they may have committed." Now in his 100th year, he has never waivered from doing his work, or living his life accordingly. From the outside, this style of understatement and non-evangelization may not seem like leadership at all. I would propose, however, that it is servant leadership at its best. The process is one of enabling, empowering all people to realize their fullest potential. It is a birthing process, a form of midwifery.

Whether looking at leadership inside or outside the Society of Friends, we need to ask, "What is the role of Spirit?" Internally, the role is much clearer, because in a Meeting setting, we all come seeking Spirit, and to act according to that guidance. Yet in either setting, wouldn't we see ourselves primarily enabling Spirit to break through? My terminology would answer with a resounding "Yes!" There is very little difference between what a Joe Gunterman does as a representative of the FCLCA, and what a Friend would do in a similar setting. Our work in the world is not to turn everybody to God, or to convince everybody to be Quakers. Our work is to build a more just, more peaceful, more loving world, and our leadership is on behalf of those causes. Our leadership and our partnerships with non-Friends can get us there.

GOSPEL ORDER IN THE 21ST CENTURY

Peggy Parsons

To be the principle listener of a listening people is hard enough when all is well. To hear the voice of God when your house is falling down on your head and your shoes are on fire is nothing short of miraculous. But I have seen it done.

Bujumbura, Burundi sits at the northern end of the deep turquoise Lake Tanganyika in Central Africa. The tranquil beauty of the lake belies the fact that at her bottom runs the Great Rift, a fault line that could rip the countryside apart with no notice. The human society thereabouts also runs deep with fault lines. Beneath an industrious, creative, and durable culture there are cycles of pain, violence, and mistrust. These things have been erupting on a regular basis for generations now.

The years 1993 to 2003 were bad. While next-door neighbor Rwanda exploded with hate and death in 1994, Burundi smoldered like a forest fire that refuses to be put out. There were hundreds of thousands of people killed in ethnic and political massacres. Every single person who lived through it was a witness to horror. The power structure in Burundi splintered into a swarm of rebel movements and coups. Bujumbura was under a nighttime curfew. Travel in the country was difficult as rebels, bandits, and sometimes government forces put up dangerous roadblocks.

The Quaker movement in Burundi started in the 1930's. David Niyonzima is the son of one of the first recorded ministers in the country. Counting anything is culturally subjective, but there are about 30,000 people attending Quaker churches in Burundi Yearly Meeting, which is affiliated with Evangelical Friends International.

David was the general secretary and legal representative of Burundi Yearly Meeting for most of the bad years. Several of them were of spent in exile in Kenya after his name appeared on death lists of educated and moderate Hutus. He barely avoided death in October of 1993 when the pastoral training school was attacked—most of his students were killed.

David was one of the people who realized that there was not going to be peace in the country until the emotional trauma was healed. He determined to get some training to start working on this problem. First he worked to deal with his own traumatization. Then, with a group of other Burundians and help from the Quaker world, he started Trauma Healing and Reconciliation Services. THARS received a grant from the USAid for work with torture survivors. Healing centers were set up in churches schools and clinics. It looked like things were going in the right direction.

The summer of 2003 was especially bad in Bujumbura. The 2000 peace talks had not brought in either of the major rebel groups, and one of these groups was sitting in the hills above Bujumbura lobbing mortars and RPGs on the town. The rebel group came into Kamenge to resupply, so running skirmishes were the norm in that suburb/slum. United Nations Helicopter gunships were targeting the rebels and occasionally whoever got in the way. The official Burundian army seemed ineffective when they weren't being criminal themselves. In late July, the United Nations pulled out all their civilians. Most western countries had emptied their embassies. I managed to show up to do some trauma healing training for THARS on August 1st of that summer.

People who are already suffering from post-traumatic stress disorder do not behave better under extreme stress. They will grab onto any possible bit of security available. Sometimes they will do pretty bad things to feel a little bit safer, a little more in control. None of us are above this.

There was turmoil in Burundi Yearly Meeting that summer. There were people who wanted a change in leadership. There were people who wanted to be in leadership, as it seemed to offer some security and control. These people could have waited until annual sessions in December and just voted Niyonzima out. (Yes, they vote.) But they did not wait. They planned a coup. They had some non-public meetings, took some non-public votes, and went to the government official in charge of recording legal representatives and changed the name. They did this without talking to Niyonzima. He found out when said official called him up to check on the paperwork. David declared the whole process invalid and called for a special yearly session. Before that could happen, the opposition took another step.

David was teaching a trauma healing session up country in Gitega. While engaged in this, the local gendarme arrived. They demanded the keys to the Yearly Meeting offices and vehicles from him. He declined to turn these over.

Now, a contextual note about the Burundian police during the bad years. They were about the least trusted people in the country. The government paid them so poorly that they freelanced. If you wanted them to investigate an actual crime such as a murder or robbery, you had to go to their station, pay for their time and transport, and bring them to the crime scene yourself. If they felt like it. If you wanted them to get involved in a purely civil matter, such as, say, church politics, the bribes would be heftier and placed higher. No one in their right mind would entrust to them important things, like keys to your truck.

David told the police that this was an internal church matter and that he would deal with it when he got back down to headquarters in Bujumbura. He was arrested on the spot. They put him into the Burundian equivalent of the drunk tank in the Gitega jail. Gitega Jail was a great place to disappear from. You go to check on your loved ones and bring them food (the only way prisoners get fed) and discover that they were never there.

Taking David in front of many witnesses, witnesses with cell phones, brought a lot of attention to the situation. Someone brought him tea and a jacket for the cool Burundian night. Gitega-based Kansas missionaries brought him blankets and let the officials know that he was known and being watched. When someone with connections got the charges transferred to the court in Bujumbura, he was finally freed on bail. The day I dropped into the country, he picked me up at the airport, apologized, and explained that he had to go to court to face trumped-up charges brought by other Quakers. He told me he was pretty sure that this would go away and that he would be home that evening—mostly sure, anyway.

The Bujumbura judge eventually ruled that this was a civil matter and dismissed the criminal charges—whatever they were.

Yearly Meeting Sessions were scheduled for the next week. The Legal Representatives of Friends from Congo and Rwanda arrived to try and mediate things. David was furious. Of course he was. He was embarrassed. He was trusting no one and nothing. He did not want to see Quaker rebels succeed in a coup d'état. It wasn't right and it wasn't seemly. The Rumor Mill—African Extra Special Edition—was working overtime. Lots of Friends presumed that something pretty stinky must be going on for such measures to be taken. Sides were being taken. Taking sides was pretty much a national pastime, often with life-and-death consequences.

I received a visitor, a local Mennonite worker who was trying to help things settle down. She told me, "David needs a friend. You don't have to be neutral. No one would believe it if you tried. Talk to him. Listen to him. And stick close. Eat where he eats—be seen eating food off his plate if you can pull it off. Travel in the same car he travels in. Your presence just might keep him safe." Then she added, "We hear a rumor that the Gitega youth group has a hand grenade and plan to fight for him at Yearly Meeting. We think this is nonsense, but we are going up early to check it out anyway. Welcome to Burundi!"

So I stayed close. And prayed and listened and did a wee bit of talking. And I watched him soften over the course of the week. He took some preparations to make sure that THARS was going to be okay, then he prepared to let go of the Yearly Meeting. By the day of the sessions, I saw a man who knew what he needed to do, who had listened and surrendered to God.

In the Great Kibimba Cathedral of Friends (okay—they don't call it that—but it's huge and cruciform—and amazing) maybe a thousand Friends gathered. The intiators of the leadership change were sitting at the head table holding the seats to which they aspired. They laid out the situation and said there would be nominations, and then a vote. The executive council met to nominate names. David's name was not allowed to be entered, even when a respected elder walked up and tried to write it on the board himself. A new Legal Representative was chosen. David's request had been that he would not fight this if he was given time to speak. Back in the church, the decision was announced. The congregation was not happy. David rose to speak. I had acquired an independent translator (turned out to be very useful.) David was calm. He did not shout (not typical Burundian Preacher style.) He smiled and laughed. He brought light to the situation. He told the people what had happened, and when. He addressed all the charges, and all the rumors, and laid them all to rest. Then he expressed hope for the Yearly Meeting and trust in God. Then he resigned.

He walked away.

He let his enemies appear to succeed.

This is not Burundian cultural normal. It is not African rebel/despot normal. One does not let go of power, nor hand it to your enemies.

But it is Gospel Order.

Because it is Christ's Church, and even the rotten apples are His apples. And sometimes you just have to step aside and let Him deal with it.

Afterwards David told me he felt free. He looked free. He had to tend to his wounds for a bit. He worshipped elsewhere for a season. But soon he was pastor of Kamenge Friends Church. Burundi Yearly meeting has survived, though it has decentralized power and formed a Kwibuka Yearly Meeting and a Kibimba Yearly Meeting. David is a well respected elder in both places.

Some of the bad actors ended up far, far away. Some ended up apologizing. Some are still working on their issues—still Jesus' problem.

The country continues to work on trauma and reconciliation issues. There are some children now who do not remember all out war. When there is peace in the house, and then peace in the school, peace in the church, then perhaps there will be a long peace in the country. We hope. We work. We let go and let God.

EVERYTHING I NEEDED TO KNOW ABOUT LEADERSHIP, I LEARNED FROM QUAKERS (AND MY MOM)

Diane Randall

Adapted from a speech delivered at
Philadelphia Yearly Meeting's 2011 Annual Sessions

THERE MAY BE readers who believe there is dissonance between Quakerism and leadership, so I want to ask you to consider three key practices of both our faith and of leadership: listening, trusting, and acting.

These three practices or qualities are so common for most Quakers as to be second nature. We don't think of these as leadership qualities, just as we probably don't think of practicing citizenship as a form of leadership. But exercising our citizenship is a way of exercising leadership. And these disciplines—listening, trusting, and acting— aren't unique to Quakers, but are pervasive throughout Quakerdom. They are disciplines that we must intentionally practice daily.

And the result of good exercise is that we get stronger when we practice. We become more powerful.

Listening

I am a convinced Quaker—convinced that the Spirit of the Divine is present in my life, convinced that the powerful love of God is meant for me and for every person, convinced that the discipline and practice of the Religious Society of Friends offers me a way to be in the world.

I had an early sense of believing in justice, not unnatural for a child. Children who are loved usually have a strong instinct for fairness. In my childhood, I was moved by the images I watched on the evening news of the war in Vietnam and the struggle for racial equality during the Civil Rights Era. The idea that our country's soldiers were killing people and being killed in a war halfway across the world for an unclear cause just wasn't rational to me, and it still isn't. People being denied equal rights based on skin color just didn't correspond with what I was learning in my Lutheran Sunday School. It was pretty clear to me that the teachings of Jesus had an answer for these injustices, and that the answer was to love our neighbors, regardless of race, nationality, religion, or creed.

My mother further taught me the truths that are effective in leading and in lobbying. Truths like, "You can win more flies with honey than with vinegar" and, "Treat others like you would like to be treated," were very popular in our house.

We weren't a politically active family. My parents voted, one a Republican and the other a Democrat, and I sometimes heard them talk about current affairs. But it wasn't until I became an adult, really until I became a mother myself, that I became politically active, joining the Nuclear Freeze Movement. Hanging around peace activists is a good way to become an engaged citizen. From those peace activists I learned that being a good citizen was more than simply voting (Of course, *all* Quakers know that), but that it included being informed, being public about our beliefs, and persuading others.

But it wasn't until I became a Friend that I learned to listen deeply, to listen to silence, to listen to the context of the speaker, and I began to understand that this type of listening is an act of love. As Friends, our practice of listening—to one another, to the Still Small Voice, to the silence—is honed through our discipline. The discipline of deep listening is how we discern, how we hear beyond the words, how we know God's presence. This is a power beyond measure.

In fact, this quality of listening that we have is what makes Friends Committee on National Legislation a powerful force for advocacy.

In my first week as FCNL's Executive Secretary, I participated in a lobby visit in Senator Reid's office with a group of eight advocates and two of Senator Reid's key staff.

The advocates were frustrated with what they perceived as lack of commitment by the Senate Democrats to protect vital human services in the Continuing Resolution of the budget, and they wanted Senator Reid to move his caucus to a stronger position. Voices grew tighter, and the tension in the room thickened. Then Ruth Flower, FCNL's Legislative Director, spoke up in her clear, knowledgeable, direct way. She not only defused the tension in the room, but also got the issue of cuts to the military budget on the table as part of the solution.

Trusting

It's not surprising that a hallmark of vitality among Friends is the level of trust within our monthly meetings and our yearly meetings. This trust doesn't come easily; we are all human and subject to the foibles of humanity, and we sometimes offend each other. But the very nature of our corporate worship is based on the trust that in our worship we are led. This is power beyond measure. It is, for me, one of the most hopeful activities I do—to sit with others, intent on being still enough to listen—and to be guided within the trust of the community.

One of the people I've had occasion to meet since coming to FCNL is Robert Levering, a Friend, who conducts *Forbes'* "100 Best Companies to Work For" survey. Major national companies vie to be listed, and Levering, and Amy Lyman have created the Great Place to Work Institute. Robert has written books and is invited to speak to business audiences around the world. Perhaps it won't surprise you that the common factor that makes companies great places to work is trust. According to the Institute, "Trust-based relationships are at the heart of every great workplace."

Lack of trust is one of the problems driving the current political debates. There is a lack of trust among political parties, between the House and the Senate, between the White House and Congress, between the Tea Party and all of government—the divisions multiply. The media loves to amplify this lack of trust. It sells, and it gives bombastic broadcasters and bloggers more to shout about.

Yet FCNL successfully builds trust; moreover, we have a legacy of integrity that comes from generations of dedicated Friends governing the organization, from our engaged activists, from our quality staff, from my predecessors—Joe Volk, Ed Snyder, and E. Raymond Wilson—and because we are Quakers.

Acting

Friends Committee on National Legislation is the most comprehensive faith-based peace and justice lobby in Washington, DC. We work closely with many colleagues. There are a lot of faith-based lobby activities: a lot of national security, human rights, peace, environmental lobbies. But I'm not aware of many that tie these issues altogether. I believe it is important for us in the future to even more effectively weave our witness in a way that makes the linkages among our programs stronger. Our world and our nation's capital are both hungry for the values we hold, for having solutions to move forward.

FCNL's call to act comes from the inspiration of Friends across the United States who give input to the policies and priorities put forward by Quaker meetings and churches. We bring a voice of hope and possibility for a world that is better than the one we inhabit. We are lifting up the inspiring vision of a world without war and the threat of war, a society with equity and justice for all, a community where every person's potential may be fulfilled, and an earth restored.

We are imagining and working in practical steps for the seemingly political impossibilities—a Congress and a foreign policy not wed to militarism; the peaceful prevention of deadly conflict; an end to nuclear weapons; reduction of greenhouse gases; an energy policy built on sustainable, renewable sources; a federal budget that is equitable and fair; protection of human rights for all.

We are engaging Friends and others who agree with us in a network of 50,000 activists and we are determined to grow that network.

We are dedicated to grounding young adults in effective leadership, citizenship, and Quaker lobbying.

Citizenship as Leadership

I want to tell you what advice and encouragement I received during my trip to the Middle East in 2011. I traveled with Jonathan Evans, who was our foreign policy legislative representative. FCNL's foreign policy program covers the world, but pays a particular attention to Israel/Palestine. The ten days we spent in Jordan, Iraq, and the occupied territories gave me a beginner's understanding of life in those places and a grounding for FCNL's work I would have never had without being there.

We had the opportunity to visit Jim and Debbie Fine, who are now working in Iraq for the Mennonite Central Committee, along with another Friend, Ann Ward. They are based in Ankawa, Iraq, just outside of Erbil. Jim is the former foreign policy legislative secretary at FCNL. He speaks Arabic and knows the Middle East from decades of experience. The visits that Jim and Debbie set up for us in Erbil and other parts of Kurdish Iraq gave us snapshots of the fragile conditions for democracy, freedom and opportunity that have captured our attention throughout the Middle East and North Africa over the past six months. Their work in peacemaking across fractious ethnic and religious divides inspired us, along with the painstaking work that local leaders are doing to build non-governmental organizations that promote effective civilian infrastructure.

Our time in Palestine—the West Bank and Gaza—was guided by Jonathan, who had lived there with his family for several years and has led Westtown school trips in the past couple of years. We spent time with Jean Zaru, Clerk of Ramallah Friends Meeting; with Kathy Bergen of the Friends International Center and a number of others active in Ramallah Friends School; the play center; AFSC; the Boycott, Divestment and Sanctions Movement, and more. We visited Bethlehem and Hebron and saw the refugee camps, and we saw the separation wall—the 25-foot concrete barrier imposed throughout neighborhoods in the West Bank. We went through the extreme checkpoint at Eretz to cross into Gaza—a dusty, impoverished strip of land packed with 1.4 million Palestinians that is as different from Tel Aviv, just 40 kilometers away, as night and day.

Palestinians and Israelis talked to us about human rights, about human dignity, about a "just peace." When we told them that our job at FCNL is to talk to the US Congress, and we asked what we should talk about, Nazim, a Gazan Palestinian said, "Tell them we're human. Tell them we're human beings."

Our visit came just days after Israeli Prime Minister Benjamin Netanyahu addressed the US Congress and received 22 standing ovations. The Palestinians were in disbelief over the seeming adoration that Congress has for a governmental leader imposing a singular agenda that thwarts the opportunities for a two-state solution for Israel and Palestine. Sam Bahour, a Palestinian business man, said to us when we asked his advice about our work with Congress, "You have your work cut out for you. There is plenty for you to do in talking with Congress."

I will end here by encouraging you to exercise your citizenship, to trust the call to leadership of being an engaged citizen and echo the words of my Palestinian friend: There is plenty of work in talking with Congress.

Don't make the mistake of talking to each other about politics and your frustrations, or about your differences with members of Congress, and think you've communicated with them. Your elected officials *need* to hear from you—even if they think they don't, or even if they dismiss you. You are a constituent; they work for you.

Trust the call to leadership, to exercise your citizenship. Be powerful beyond measure.

DISCERNMENT IN ACTION

Stephen McNeil

> *I pin my hopes on quiet processes and small circles*
> *in which vital and transforming events take place.*
> *-Rufus Jones*

WHEN I was young, Adelphi Friends Meeting in Maryland gave me many opportunities to serve the meeting. I was given a clerking responsibility at a young age, and supported through life-changing experiences that taught me both organizational skills and how much responsibility I could take on. Elders taught me how to take minutes at the Peace & Social Order Committee, get up and speak at Meeting for Worship on the Occasion of Business, and most importantly how to listen carefully, let go of my personal agenda, and be patient as Spirit moved decisions often away from my preconceived desires–in short, how to appreciate discernment in action.

In this I sometimes failed, but I was encouraged to continue. For instance, during the calls for our meeting to join in Vietnam demonstrations, some members or their spouses were military or ex-military and felt uncomfortable about agreeing to this corporate witness. Often the discomfort delayed a decision. I felt most impatient. But listening and struggling with these other viewpoints led to a stronger decision to go forward as a group to the demonstration, and to respond with respect to those in uniform, something that my college classmates did not always do.

When I was 18 I attended the session of Baltimore Yearly Meeting where Friends of two different traditions who had split years ago were meeting together in session for the first time. Sitting next to two elderly women, I heard them time and again state about various speakers during a business session, "He's not a Quaker" or, "She's not a Quaker." The speakers were convinced Friends or liberal Friends. Finally, my Irish American upbringing got the better of me and I turned to them and said: "Should I kiss thy holy feet that you were born Quaker?" Quickly I felt a pair of hands behind me on my shoulders and the unknown-to-me elder (at 18, practically everyone was an elder) took me aside and pointed out the indelicate nature of my comments at a time when all were struggling to have a reunified Yearly Meeting. I got his point, and felt no rancor—or rather felt the truth of his eldering. I acted more properly thereafter.

For seven years, beginning when I was 21, I served on AFSC's Pretrial Justice Program Committee in Washington, DC. Our focus was pushing for structural changes in the DC jail and the Women's Bureau of Detention. We conducted annual surveys with inmates there to determine our goals for the coming year. One small act that took no little effort was to get an industrial fan into the jail in the summertime. Prior to this the heat was intolerable in the fortress-like structure. This service brought me into contact with a fine mentor, AFSC Program Director Bernice Just (who eventually became a Friend), an incredible African American woman who led many reforms in DC's justice system. She showed me how steadily pursuing documentation over time of the abuses in the system, reflecting with others on the Program Committee on what changes were possible, and then pushing those through the political process was part of a collective discernment that led to meaningful bail reforms. While we engaged in pure service in the jails, we also did the hard work of dealing with the politics of change. Service without political advocacy can be incomplete.

During this same period, my meeting had a member who was doing two years at Petersburg (VA) Federal Prison for draft resistance. He and another Quaker conscientious objector requested that Friends come in and hold Meeting for Worship. I had turned in my draft card, and felt some responsibility to respond to his request. I ended up as the coordinator. Over the course of six years, more than 500 Friends from five Monthly Meetings went into the prison and conducted a weekly meeting service.

In this time another Quaker elder came into my life and mentored me: Fay Honey Knopp, who was serving as a Prison Visitors Service (PVS) staffer. Through her encouragement, we created a halfway house, Puddledock, for prison visitors–mostly wives, children, and girlfriends–that lasted for five years. Time and again I saw how Honey handled the prison warden on issues of discrimination, sexism, and unfair treatment while honoring him with respect as a person. Through an internship with the Friends Committee on National Legislation, I worked with her on testimony for changes before a Congressional Committee oversight hearing on the Federal Bureau of Prisons. In the back and forth of crafting her testimony–and in her delivery–I again saw her weighing and choosing–discerning–which experiences she would relate to the Committee and for what changes she would advocate on behalf of Friends.

One small act of service that our meeting adopted during the Civil Rights era was to provide clothing and financial support for a group of African American women who were civil rights leaders in Indianola, Mississippi. In the early 1970s, the "Circle of Forty" (donors) had collected some clothing in their annual drive.

Two non-Friends and I were sent down to Indianola to deliver the clothes and to touch base with the women. I had some fears, being then a long-haired, bearded youth traveling with two Jews in Mississippi, but our trip was uneventful until one evening. The women we had come to support, good Baptists, got into a conversation with us on the second evening of our stay about exactly how did Friends baptize. The non-Friends looked to me for an answer. I realized from the question that the women probably had no real idea who the Friends were. I also knew, having attended school with mostly African American Protestants, including Pentecostals, that this was a serious question.

I went quiet for a bit in prayer.

Then I said clearly that Quakers did not believe in water baptism. Their shocked faces and quiet did not surprise me. I dug deeper and told them that Friends did believe in the power of the Spirit and living from that power. They smiled. One replied, "Then you believe in the Pentecost, in the Holy Spirit's baptism by fire, not water." I reckoned that there was more than an element of truth in that and nodded my head in agreement. We ended the evening contented. I felt satisfied that I had not spoken beyond my Guide and that I had fulfilled my responsibility to Truth, and engaged in a moment of discernment.

Whether it was waiting to move forward, not speaking, or speaking up with convincement, my times of discernment in action all made me feel more confident. I was able to take risks that I don't think I would have taken without that period of reflection, listening, and convincement. And the corporate involvement of my Quaker community, both meetings and organizations like AFSC and FCNL, sustained me in my witness over a much longer period of time than I would have been capable of on my own.

A MINISTRY OF PRESENCE

Bill and Genie Durland

G ENIE AND I have been together almost as long as we have been Quakers, about 40 years. My first contact with Quakers, while still a Catholic pacifist activist, was as a subscriber to the Wider Quaker Fellowship and sometime attender at a Quaker meeting in Virginia in 1970. Genie was one of those people who was a Quaker before she even knew it. When she was a 6th-grader, she wrote a reflection dedicated to her grandmother:

> To my Grandmother, Who is Always a Friend to Everyone.
> Be Friends with all your foes, and cast away your woes.
> For triumph meets you here, with peace, nothing you should fear.
> If everyone on earth were friends, you'd find that every country blends.
> In olden times our fathers fought.
> War would bring lasting peace, they thought.
> In olden days or modern times it is never good to fight.
> A land can have more happiness, not using all its might.
> And that is just a simple rule, 'Always be friends.'

As Jesus said, before the peace comes division (Luke 51-59) and our first experiences together were just that, some of our own making and some of the violence of the world. But for surviving the tribulation there is a saving promise, and so we were joined together forever and for future callings.

102

All that we have been part of originated in a spiritual reflection, resulting in the radical witness of Quakers and other people of conscience. We have heard the call to community over and over in our lives, and have expressed it through public service with those who spoke truth to power. Bill was one of the founders of the Community for Creative Nonviolence in Washington, D.C., and together with others we were founders of the Matthew 25 Free Medical Clinic and Center for Nonviolence in Ft. Wayne, Indiana. With Genie's leadership, we also formed a retreat center that we hoped would eventually be a "Pendle Hill West." From 1989-93, Quakers and peace activists from around the country refreshed themselves at our Erimias Community Retreat Center in rural Cokedale, Colorado.

Witness Against War

It took a very spiritual, relational-but-down-to-earth Quaker elder to be the catalyst for the activism of the National Center on Law and Pacifism, which Bill, Genie, and Father Richard McSorley created in 1978. Bob Anthony of Media, Pennsylvania, was a World War II conscientious objector and subsequent Quaker convert. Each year, he refused to pay the percentage of his income taxes comparable to the annual federal budget allocation for militarism and war. He wound up in tax court, justifying his refusal to pay on the grounds that what he was doing was nothing more than what he did as a conscientious objector to serving in the military. He now saw that paying for war was an even greater threat to peace, creating weapons of mass destruction, and thereby a greater burden on his conscience.

Bob was introduced to us earlier by a Quaker woman who was part of the Churchmouse Collective, the religious arm of the Movement for a New Society. We had met her in Philadelphia in 1977, when we moved there and she asked us to consider offering legal representation to Quakers and others whose consciences led them to resist war taxes. She said that there had been no available sympathetic and low-cost lawyer representing this movement for some time, or anyone who could take up the leadership of it both legally and spiritually.

In order to do such work, we knew we needed time for reflection, and a community to provide clarity and organization to process the calling. We wanted our lives to be spiritually situated to be able to speak truth to the powers that be. Out of those desires, the Center on Law and Pacifism was born and Anthony's case was carried all the way to the Supreme Court, where Bill argued that Anthony's free exercise of religion had been infringed upon.

A hearing on his case was denied, but a formidable record was made, and Anthony inspired us all to resist war taxes—a witness the two of us continue to this day. Anthony's Supreme Court case was followed by three others there involving two Quakers, a Catholic worker, and an Episcopal priest. Genie published that witness with the creation of *Center Peace*, the Center's news magazine, and a guidebook was written early on as war tax resisters all over the country began to receive counseling and representation. The Center added cases of conscientious objection to war and representation for the impoverished and the imprisoned, whose needs fell between the cracks of poverty and prison laws.

And so it was for ten years, ending only after we opened up a western branch of the Center in Colorado Springs. Upon our return to Colorado, Bill devoted ten years to teaching at a community college in the city of Trinidad, in the most economically depressed part of Colorado. It is peopled largely by the remnants of Native American and Spanish minority groups.

Ministry of Presence in Palestine

We discovered yet another calling in 2001 to provide a "ministry of presence" in Palestine. Our understanding of this particular witness was shaped by the experiences of Quakers Dyke Vermilye and his wife Avis, whom we knew from time at Pendle Hill and who had spent time in Zimbabwe; and by Jean Zaru, Clerk of Ramallah Friends Meeting in Palestine. Being there to experience the oppression firsthand and live subject to the same abuses and restrictions that define the lives of Palestinians under occupation was the heart of our ministry of presence. It gives Palestinians hope that others in the world might understand their plight, and gives them partners in their own acts of resistance.

By this time, we had been longtime members of the Lamb's Community Worship Group of the Albuquerque Monthly Meeting and Intermountain Yearly Meeting. With various clearness committee meetings assisting us, and after prayer and reflection, we were strongly led to the ravaged countryside of the Palestinian military occupation. Our calling was to provide several things: assistance, accompaniment, and advocacy, but essentially we were witnessing, which is different from protesting or demonstrating. Those practices are concerned with what "works" or is effective at creating particular outcomes. Witnessing is about accompanying the oppressed and speaking truth to power, whether it is effective or not.

The impetus for this calling came through the Christian Peacemaker Teams. Since 1988, this organization, founded by a coalition of historic peace churches—Mennonites, Brethren and Friends United Meeting Quakers—has brought a ministry of presence to the victimized people in Israel and Palestine. Acts of violent and brutal oppression regularly occur in Palestinian neighborhoods under the Israeli military occupation. The ministry of presence is accomplished by "getting in the way,"—a risky practice of walking into tense scenes of conflict and literally getting between those on the verge of violence. This witness reminded us that the early Christians were first known as "The Way" and that pacifist religious activism has caused many to lose their lives (and certainly their comfort) for conscience's sake.

During 2001 to 2010, we made five trips to the Middle East, including Jordan, Egypt, Iraq, Israel, and especially the occupied West Bank and the Israeli-blockaded Gaza Strip. These trips were made possible by many Quaker meetings, individual Quakers, members of the historic peace churches, and other conscientious people who paid the costs of our travels. Often, we were "in harm's way," as is said of the military but in our case, as unarmed witnesses for peace and justice. As we expected, we were sometimes targets of mortar fire, tear gas, and detention while joining Palestinians in what is known as accompaniment, to be with them when physical attack is threatened, or when aid or protection was needed in that war zone.

In the case of Christian Peacemaker Teams the leadership is provided by those we serve. CPTers never go into a zone of lethal conflict as American ambassadors seeking to provide our understanding of the help needed. We go only where invited, and then act only according to the stated needs of our hosts.

On one occasion, a fruit vendor in Hebron's old city was assaulted by Israeli soldiers because he failed to respond quickly enough to a curfew announcement. His stand was destroyed and he was injured badly enough to need a trip to the hospital. Upon his return to the area, soldiers would not allow him to go home, visible from where we stood with him, while his wife and children waited. They said a Jewish funeral procession was expected to be coming through so the Palestinian could not be where he was. We intervened with the soldiers, with whom Bill was able to relate from his pre-pacifist military service. They finally relented and and let the Palestinian pass with no funeral procession in sight.

Another time, as we waited in a long line in the hot sun to pass through the checkpoint at Qalandia (between Jerusalem and Ramallah), we noticed a young mother holding a crying child who was clearly sick. The temperature was over 100 degrees, and we feared for the baby's life. So Bill moved to the edge of the line and called for the nearest soldier to come over to him and asked him to move the mother and baby to the front of the long line. The soldier said he could do nothing, so Bill asked to speak to his superior, who subsequently ordered the soldier to allow them to move. This is an example of the impact international observers can have in such situations if they take simple actions.

Accompaniment also meant helping farmers harvest crops in fields that lie so close to illegal Israeli settlements that settlers often shoot at them. The hope is always that the sight of identifiable internationals will deter the settlers and allow farmers to bring in grapes, plums, and other crops that are their livelihood. We were told next time the settlers would shoot to kill, but with CPT red hats held high, we saw no settlers.

During our first tour of duty with CPT in the West Bank, we were invited by Palestinians in the city of Beit Jala to act as human shields by sleeping in various Palestinian homes suffering mortar fire from the adjacent Israeli settlement. Our presence was announced on local radio and TV, but it did not stop the mortar fire. However, on that particular night no Palestinian homes were destroyed, so we believe the shelling was purposely less accurate.

While on "active duty" with CPT we organized and led a largely Quaker fact-finding delegation that included a visit to the Ramallah Friends School and overnights with Ramallah families, including parents of children at the school. We were led to violate the military-imposed curfew there to complete our duties, and brought our delegation out unharmed.

Significance is Success

Quaker leadership in our lives can be summed up as a response to
need as defined by those in need. In the case of the work of the Center
on Law and Pacifism, Bill repeatedly went to court at several levels
to argue the conscientious cases of religious war tax resisters. The
expectation of both lawyer and client was not to "win" in secular terms,
not to somehow beat the IRS, not to seek effectiveness, but rather
significance. It was to use the court as a forum for witness, in which
case the process was always a winner. In its own way this work was also
a ministry of presence—the presence of a pacifist lawyer in the courts.

In our work in Palestine, our calling was to be of service to the cause
of the beleaguered Palestinians. The lessons we've learned have been
more about the courage and determination of countless conscientious
objectors and of Palestinian families, mothers, children, farmers,
school teachers, trying to live life as normally as possible. The
Palestinians we've worked with have been almost always nonviolent
and have continually sought to find ways to apply Gandhi's principles
in their struggle. They know that nonviolent resistance gives them the
moral high ground. But this part of their story never seems to appear
in American media, so our second most important role has been to
tell their story for them. We are just grateful to have been able to be a
small part of their struggle.

During one of our visits to Ramallah we were fortunate to attend
Meeting for Worship with Ramallah Friends. At the rise of meeting,
Clerk Jean Zaru thanked us for our "ministry of presence." For us it
was the most meaningful moment in all our work there.

Leadership
in Quaker Organizations

Joe Volk
Shan Cretin &
Lucy Duncan
Doug Bennett

IN THE EARLIER SECTIONS of this book, we reflected on the fundamental aspects of Quaker leadership: listening, discerning, and acting. The interrelationships between each of these three are so plentiful that it's difficult to talk about one without mentioning the others in the same breath. These remain central to leadership within Quaker organizations—or even in secular organizations committed to equality, as the authors here are quick to point out.

But there are numerous paradoxical challenges to leading and working within the organizations founded by Quakers to do work in the wider world. Joe speaks to his years of experience trying to lead while "in the world but not of the world," a phrase common among Friends, while also obeying George Fox's direction to "walk cheerfully over the Earth, answering that of God in everyone." Lucy and Shan address the paradox of leadership that is willing to take risks and admit wrongdoing, while also seeking a sense of the collective direction of those being led by the Spirit. Too often, Quaker leaders can find they are "tall poppies," at risk of having their (metaphorical) heads chopped off. And Doug speaks directly to the very real challenges of being a leader when faced with the Quaker tendency to look askance at the leaders charged with the care and safekeeping of so many treasured institutions.

Paradoxes are powerful teaching tools. Though these Friends speak from years of experience working for Quaker organizations, the gentle criticism and advice they offer are such that each of us should take heed. It can just as easily apply in our meetings and churches, and in the secular aspects of our lives.

Queries on Leading in Quaker Organizations

What paradoxes do you see in leading a contemporary organization according to Quaker principles?

From the perspective of a Quaker, what do you think it means to support a leader? How do you feel we fail to support our leaders?

How might you seek to lead from a place of listening to the Spirit while also attending to the practical, day-to-day needs of an organization?

QUAKER MANAGEMENT?

Joe Volk

Adapted from a talk given at
Earlham School of Religion's 2011 Leadership Conference

I FEEL considerable humility as I try to address the topic of Quaker leadership. You should know that I am a practitioner, not a theologian and not a scholar, of Quaker leadership. Nor do I consider myself an expert on Quaker management. Many of my past colleagues will assure you that I am no genius.

If I know anything about this topic, it comes from nearly forty years of on the job training. I made a lot of mistakes over those years, and I hope that I have learned some lessons along the way. For whatever reasons, Friends have extended to me the privilege of playing leadership roles at the American Friends Service Committee (AFSC), where I served 18 years, and at the Friends Committee on National Legislation (FCNL), where I served 21 years.

In those roles, I was able to try out ways of managing a Quaker operation while being supported and guided by mentors and committees. I had faithful, seasoned, and smart role models and mentors—women and men—who nurtured me. A number of them had gone through powerful annealing experiences that prepared them to be effective servant-leaders. From the labor organizer in the Appalachian coal fields to combatants in the Pacific Theater and military occupation of Hiroshima after the A-bomb, to the entrepreneur who built a billion dollar business, or one called to feed the hungry in Biafra, these people provided me with an uncommon and precious opportunity to learn, right at the beginning of my career.

At the same time, playing a role as a Quaker leader was challenging and sometimes difficult. It can be lonely. After my 21 years at FCNL, I was able to say to our General Committee, "Thank you for allowing me to serve as your Executive Secretary for 21 years, they have been 15 wonderful years, indeed!"

Leadership, management, and administration are often conflated. They're related but not the same. However, in my experience, all three involve a ministry that supports and enables others to address the primary purposes of the organization.

A Quaker Paradox

Quaker leaders can be a long time in the making. My first significant encounter with Friends came—oddly or predictably—in 1968 when, as an infantry rifleman in a mechanized cavalry unit, I refused, for reasons of conscience, to go with my combat unit to Vietnam. Friends supported me through the military counseling work of the AFSC in Denver.

My first job in a Friends organization started in 1972 at AFSC's Southeast Regional Office, where I did nonviolence training and action work. Not until 1984 did I write my letter seeking membership in the Religious Society of Friends, where I had found my spiritual home. Looking back on my contact with Friends, I see that I was absorbing a paradox.

When in the early 1970s I asked a North Carolina Yearly Meeting-Conservative Friend, Cal Geiger, "Who are the Quakers?" Cal replied without a moment's hesitation, "We Friends are a peculiar people not conformed to this world." That conveyed to me that Friends would be separate from the world, standing aside from it.

I said, "But aren't Friends called to walk cheerfully over the earth answering that of God in everyone? Isn't that the way Friends were called to 'preach Christ?'" Cal replied simply, "Yes, that's also true."

I wondered, how can Friends stand away from this world and also deeply engage this world?

Over my years at work for AFSC and for FCNL, that conversation with Cal and the stories of my mentors have informed my work, that is, my religious practice. We're a peculiar people not conformed to this world, and we're called into this world to answer that of God in everyone.

The Oxymoron of Quaker Management

We've heard and enjoyed oxymorons for years. We put together two words with contrary meanings and chuckle. During the U.S. war in Vietnam, many peace activists used the phrase "military intelligence" as a derogatory term and got laughs. At the height of the U.S. airline industry—when they served meals on flights—passengers chuckled at the term "airline food."

Why might "Quaker management" similarly amuse us? Perhaps because Friends have a bottom-up society and polity, and management is perceived as a top-down directorate. Can a religious society that eschews doctrine and holds that each and every member of its society may lead in ministry at some time also employ management of its organizations? How could management and the Quaker way of free thinking and acting be compatible?

To me, the key goal of Quaker management is to maintain an organization's integrity with the vision of Friends through holding the paradoxical tension between being "a peculiar people not conformed to this world" and "walking cheerfully in the world answering that of God in everyone." This is true in whatever Friends organization—service agency, lobby group, education institution, Friends meeting, or Friends church.

Answering to God requires that we first find God, and then listen, as Douglas Steere said. Do we find God under the roof of the church or outside the church in the world of human events? Maybe both, but in my experience, out in the world trumps under the roof.

Practice as Faith

As I understand the experience of Friends, the bloody English civil wars of the 17th Century moved a number of seekers to discover the practices that gave birth to what is now the Religious Society of Friends. At that time of deadly conflict, adherence to doctrine (asserting beliefs) and competition among doctrines literally resulted in God's children killing each other in the name of Jesus.

Beliefs seduced people to kill other people. Such killing could not be the will of God. So Friends could not assert beliefs; they rejected doctrine. They turned instead to practice. Love was the first motion for all practice of faith. This motion of love moved Friends out from under the roof of the church and into the world of human events where God was active—and is still active today.

Here was—and is—Quaker theological genius at work: freedom from established religion brings us into a closer relationship to the Divine, and that closer relationship to the divine happens through work in the world—through the practice of faith—that expresses God's love for all creation. Getting closer to God means getting closer to all that God created. Paradoxically, everyday practice becomes the venue for our spiritual life, and liturgical practices of established religions risk becoming the icy fingers of death.

God cares about what we do, and what we do leads us toward or away from the Divine. Seekers after God take the risk to go out into the world. We are pulled into the world of human events by the first motion, love. We risk error and suffering to practice hope in a hopeless world. Our practice of hope brings hope—The Light—into the world. We become partners with the divine process of creation.

Quaker Management and Vision

We don't always succeed at maintaining integrity with our Quaker vision. Sometimes we fall down. "We fall down; we get up," as the gospel song says.

It's also fair to say that we sometimes succeed. We might ask—in another place and at another time—when have we seen well-managed Friends' organizations succeed at maintaining integrity with their Quaker vision? We might make a list of projects that seemed to work well in this regard. We might then ask questions about each of these. For example, did the management compete with or contribute to that success? Did the vision eschew good management or did it beg for it?

Awhile ago, I was having lunch with John Kirksey, the Executive Director of The National Multicultural Institute. I tuned into his remark that, "Having good management is not sufficient. Having a culture of inclusion is not sufficient, either. A healthy organization will seek a well managed organization that supports a culture of inclusion." I think he is right, and that pattern may hold also for Quaker vision and Quaker management. Neither is sufficient by itself; we need both. Most Friends will say they have a concept of Quaker vision, but many will ask, "What is Quaker management?"

In my experience, such a thing as Quaker management does exist and can work. However—despite what numerous Friends and observers may believe— Friends' organizations operate under the same laws of gravity as non-Quaker organizations. Therefore, Quaker management, in my view, incorporates many best practices of the nonprofit and the for-profit worlds.

Here are five sets of questions that I used in my role as a manager in a Quaker organization and that have served me well.

Governing
"Is the board governing? Are we the staff implementing?"

In the context that we live in a governed universe and try to follow divine leadings, Friends organizations are governed by named groups of people whose job it is to discern those leadings for us in our times. Simply put, the board governs, the executive director is accountable to the board, and the staff implement, and volunteers — even if they are members of the board — are accountable to staff when serving as volunteers.

Decision making
"Are we submitting ourselves to the Quaker process for discernment? Are we inviting all, including staff, into the ministry?"

Board decisions are made in meetings for worship with a concern for business, using a Quaker consensus decision-making process. Staff decision-making process is more hierarchical, with the executive having final say. Smart and effective businesses and nonprofits use a consensus building processes to reach staff level decisions. Why? Because our staff and the experience of our staff members bring a rich pool of information, understanding, and creative ideas to our organization.

Budget
"Are we using the budget as a planning tool?"

The budget is a planning tool, not a constraint. The board, i.e. the governors, use the budget for strategic planning as well as for guidance on annual allocation of resources. The budget should be at the service of organizational goals, and those goals should be identified by the governors and limited in number. One of the weaknesses of organizations is undercapitalization. We need a capital budget, and we need an operating budget. We need realistic budgets.

Spending
"Am I being true to our donors?"

Our Friends organizations depend upon the free-will giving of our constituents. Uppermost in the mind of the board, the executive, and the staff should be the question: are we using the contributors' dollars...

... for the purposes stated?
... in an effective and efficient manner?

That is, are we keeping good faith with our donors? Whenever I felt a doubt about how or how much to spend, I imagined actual donors sitting at my desk with me, and I asked myself, "Would she or he be comfortable with this decision to spend these contributed dollars?"

Staff time

"Are we focused on the primary purposes of our organization?"
"Are we using staff time to advance the primary purposes of the organization?"

Whenever I had a scheduling conflict and whenever our staff asked me, "Joe, should I do A or should I do B?" I stopped to ask myself this question: Which of these activities advances the primary purposes of our organization? Sometimes both, but more often one stood out.

Regarding the Executive Director's time, I tried to ask, "Am I using the time of this senior role in our organization to do what only the Executive Director can do and not duplicating what others can (and should) do?"

It is also worth noting that doubt ministers to faith. The role of doubt in good management of Quaker organizations is underappreciated. Doubt helps us to refine our planning and to open ourselves to continuing revelation.

What's Quaker Vision?

We've all heard the phrase, "Without a vision the people perish." On the other hand, without the people the vision doesn't matter.

New research seems to validate Friends' practice of testing leadings in a community of seekers; in experiments, groups of people, rather than charismatic or expert individuals, were more likely to get the right answers to unknowns. Yes, exceptions happen. Sometimes the group needs a conscience-driven individual.

When groups of Friends engage in problem-solving out in the world with care and concern for others, Friends rediscover the promise of the Gospels of entry into a "now-but-not-yet world" that gives us a hint what the Kingdom of God would be.

When we describe that "now-but-not-yet world," we produce a vision that is distinctively Quaker and yet universal, another paradox. That's why so many who are not Friends become attracted to the work of Friends.

To express our Friends' vision, we need a narrative that tells our story. That story reminds us and tells others what our purpose is. FCNL has such a story. FCNL was blessed that one of our clerks could gather the sense of our General Committee in a poetic manner. She tested whether Friends could unite in this statement of purpose:

> We seek a world free of war and the threat of war.
> We seek a society with equity and justice for all.
> We seek a community where every person's potential may be fulfilled.
> We seek an earth restored.

Our General Committee did unite with our clerk, and FCNL's story is now captured in that brief narrative. One reason FCNL has been able to work in an effective manner and remain true to our General Committee's vision has been that the General Committee has so clearly translated the Good News of the Gospel stories into an accessible and compelling story for our times.

In closing, I'll say that I've seen four pillars of a visionary Friends organization:

A Vision: the story or the narrative grounded in the Good News of the Gospels.

The Culture of Inclusion: distinctively Quaker and yet accessible to all, i.e. universal.

A Plan: how we move from the problem to the solution, remembering that "love is the first motion."

Quaker Management: relying on best practices and practicing a ministry of support that enables work.

Is "Quaker Management" an oxymoron? No. Is it genius at work? Yes, I think so.

TAKING THE RISKS OF FAITH: LEADERSHIP IN A QUAKER CONTEXT

Shan Cretin and Lucy Duncan

Is Quaker leadership an oxymoron? Leading, by one definition, requires establishing a goal or direction and influencing others to follow. Leaders are often praised for being visionary, for seeing possibilities that are not yet widely understood. In times of crisis, leadership may call for prompt action, and for making controversial decisions that by their nature cannot be delayed.

Amongst Friends, we believe that all of us have gifts and leadings to contribute. And so we ask our clerks for something that seems on its face rather different from traditional visions of leadership: to seek out the will of the body and to seek unity with the Spirit, so no one of us stands out in front of others. Martha Paxson Grundy has written of visionary Quaker leaders who, like the tall poppy, risk having his or her head chopped off.

Based on our experiences within and outside of Friends' organizations, we have come to see that authentic leadership, whether secular or Quaker, draws on many of the same principles. Difficulties arise when, as John Coleman recently pointed out in *Friends Journal*, our Quaker practices become undisciplined and fail to value the expertise required to discern complex questions. Honoring gifts and leadings is an important part of inviting the community to discern the collective call for powerful action that aligns with our understanding of spiritual truth. In the case of decisions with weight, that usually means that some Friends, perhaps all of us, will be walking outside of our comfort zone.

The Origins of AFSC's Distinct Ministry

The American Friends Service Committee was founded on principles of visionary Quaker leadership, as Rufus Jones described, "in the sharp crisis of 1917, when the first steps of faith were taken." Jones, Henry Cadbury, and the other founders were seeking a way for young Friends to contribute to peace, as an alternative to military service, at a time when Quakers were divided, over both theology and the peace testimony. The brilliance of their leadership was in recognizing the deeper truth that even those Friends who were not pacifists could unite around the need for compassionate action aimed at the human beings caught up in the conflict. So the Service Committee was founded as a faith-based organization that did not proselytize its fractured faith, but only asked to be judged on its deeds.

Our Quaker history often represents the courageous acts of a few visionary Friends as collective acts that were uncontroversial and universally supported within our community. Actually most Quaker prophets were fairly marginalized at the time of their witness. As is well documented in *Fit for Freedom, not for Friendship*, Lucretia Mott, John Woolman and other abolitionists were often isolated within their Quaker meetings.

By the early 1920's AFSC had begun to recognize the deep roots of violence in American and Quaker society, especially around issues of race. What could be done to address the ongoing mistreatment of Native Americans, the unfinished work to free African-Americans from the continued legacy of slavery, and draconian immigration laws targeting "undesirables" such as Asians, Mexicans and Italians? Since the formation of the first Interracial Section in 1924, AFSC has continued to grapple with the question of how a Quaker organization can rightly engage with communities of color in the United States and around the world to end the racism and the "exceptionalism" that permeates our lives. Grounded in the peace testimony, "AFSC staffers [came] to see race problems not just as the result of flawed individuals but as the result of flawed institutions as well..."

Offering effective leadership around issues of race continues to be much more challenging than offering such leadership on peace.

The Service Committee still straddles the gap between the views of the Quaker community and communities of color, both inside the organization between the diverse staff and largely Quaker board, and outside in the communities and Quaker meetings with whom we partner. In November 2012, the American Friends Service Committee (AFSC) approved a new mission statement that seeks to embrace openly the tension between being Quaker and fully honoring the diversity of the world in which we work:

The AFSC is a Quaker organization that promotes lasting peace with justice, as a practical expression of faith in action. Drawing on continuing spiritual insights and working with people of many backgrounds, we nurture the seeds of change and respect for human life that transform social relations and systems.

How do we lead an organization whose mission is foundational systemic and societal change? This question lies close to the central mission of the Religious Society of Friends: How do we lead within a faith community that at its core is working to comprehend, reveal, and create the Kingdom of God on earth, understanding that this can only be co-created nonviolently in community?

Like a good clerk, we must begin by articulating and testing our understanding with those we ask to share and act on our vision:

Peace must rest on the presence of justice. The violence of poverty is as abhorrent and more pernicious than physical violence and falls unequally on people of color. We still live in a world in which the exploitation of communities of color benefits those with power and wealth, those of European descent.

It's a deep calling that AFSC and Friends carry into our homes and communities, what else is more worth dedicating our hearts and minds to pursue? For AFSC and the Religious Society of Friends to work to make visible healed and sustainable communities, there must be among us people courageous enough take the risks of leadership. When we have unity on the leading, we must be ready to take the next step and begin to experiment with deeds that will carry our message into action.

Taking action in the world inevitably means taking risks, making mistakes, and hopefully learning from those errors. Continuing revelation, like the scientific method, requires us to be willing to experiment and to be willing to celebrate when we discover we are wrong because this is the path that will bring us closer to the truth. The best leaders in the secular world also understand that experimentation and testing ideas is an important way that individuals and organizations learn and improve.

Acknowledging Aspirations and Truths

The gaps between who we aspire to be and the truth of where we are and how we are is the place where transformation can occur, but it can't happen if we cling so tightly to our idea of ourselves that we are unwilling to acknowledge the mistakes of the past and live into a future with more integrity, clarity, and power.

AFSC has sometimes been painfully slow to correct our own inevitable mistakes. When Bayard Rustin, the gay organizer who worked side-by-side with Martin Luther King, Jr. to organize The March on Washington and who worked for AFSC for a period, was arrested in 1953 for "sexual misconduct," some in leadership in the organization wanted him to remove his name as an author of *Speak Truth to Power: a Quaker Search for an Alternative to Violence*. This important pamphlet sought "to give practical demonstration to the effectiveness of love in human relations," and was a major statement of Christian pacifism. There were several other leaders within AFSC willing to support Rustin and fight to keep his name on the publication, but in the end Rustin relented to the pressure and asked for his name to be removed. It was wrong, and this error was only acknowledged and corrected in 2010.

Why do we sometimes take so long to act? In Quaker meetings we are used to waiting to discern until all are easy with a decision; we expect that we can wait for clarity on God's guidance. Yet in our meetings and our Quaker organizations, some decisions have stark fiscal and strategic consequences that make it difficult to take the view, "We're Quakers, we'll talk about it until we agree. Then we'll act." We are aware of the risks of wrong action, but not acting can also be a form of wrong action, with deep risks and dire consequences.

One consequence of inaction is that we lose the opportunity to learn from trying. Praying, thinking, and imagining can only take us so far. We need the information from experience in order to really know what might work. Inward reflection and understanding are important, but so is testing those understandings not only in threshing sessions or through consultation, but also through experimentation. When George Fox said, "This I knew experimentally" he laid down an important cornerstone of our faith. Unity or sense of the meeting doesn't mean everyone is equally happy or agrees this is the best choice. It does mean that those who have doubts in the particular path also have faith that we will test the decision, evaluate it, and correct it if it doesn't work.

We offer here, based on experience and reflection, the principles and practices that we have gleaned from our own experiments and by drawing on the wisdom of other Quaker, faith-based, and secular sources. Like all such advices, these are incomplete and evolving as we continually test and learn.

Articulate a shared vision - People choose to work in Quaker organizations because they feel a calling to the mission and vision of that body. However, a personal passion for the mission can become a problem if staff allow their personal leadings to get in the way of planning and coordinating with others across the organization to fulfill its purpose. A leader's role is to listen carefully and to articulate a compelling shared vision towards which people are motivated to work. The organizational vision must reflect more than the leader's personal agenda. Through active listening, a leader can shape a vision that encompasses the personal aspirations of staff, volunteers and the broader communities served. People are much more willing to subordinate their personal agendas when they see that it is possible to achieve common, powerful outcomes by working together, far exceeding what any one person can accomplish alone.

At the beginning of the process to develop AFSC's new strategic plan, a group of staff from across the organization came together to describe a shared vision/framework for lasting peace. Once the small initial group had come to unity on a document, small, diverse groups throughout AFSC came together by phone to discuss the principles and ideas in that framework. That document and those conversations became the basis for the new long term plan, and the plan which arises from that shared vision.

Create clarity - Effective leadership depends upon establishing clear roles, processes, and expectations. Transparency is critical so that everyone can function with a shared understanding of the organizational context. It is neither critical nor helpful to have everyone weigh in on every decision—a practice that can quickly paralyze the organization. An effective leader, Quaker or otherwise, is best served by defining who has authority for what, delegating decisions to the people closest to the work, and trusting others to fulfill their role. Doug Bennett asked a question regularly at Earlham: "Whose decision is this and as a consequence of what process?" It's a question that all Quaker leaders should ask regularly and answer forthrightly.

Experiment and learn - A spirit of experimentation and a willingness to take risks is essential for all organizations. Yes, it's important to season decisions in the Light, and through consultation, but it's also important to recognize that most decisions will not be perfect and that one important way to listen is to attend to what happens when something is tried out for the first time.

In order for an atmosphere of experimentation to thrive, those with power must be quick to own their own mistakes and make corrections promptly. All staff must feel safe to reach for stretch goals, try new ideas, and to learn from one another. It's important to hold people accountable for demonstrating learning and by not repeating mistakes, but if staff are reprimanded for missteps, they won't learn. Help staff understand how to conduct experiments in a thoughtful, controlled way by articulating anticipated outcomes in advance, explicitly stating the logic by which the actions could lead to those outcomes, and reporting back honestly on the experience. An organization must be willing to recalibrate new approaches based on thoughtful analysis.

Listen – Of course, listening is key to effective leadership in any organization, but especially within Quaker organizations. Listen to your Inner Guide daily and regularly. Listen to the people most involved and closest to the situation. In the case of AFSC, we create and implement most of our programs working hand-in-hand with our community partners. We operate from the understanding that those in the community have knowledge and resources that are essential to building effective solutions to the problems they face. This same lesson applies when designing processes or addressing problems inside the organization: If those most directly impacted are not involved in shaping a solution, success is unlikely.

Learn from others – Discernment requires both an informed mind and an open heart. Sometimes Quakers rely too much on their inner Light, losing the chance to learn from the experience or expertise of others. Finding out how people inside and outside the world of Friends approach organizational structure, personnel matters, finances, or programs can inform our work and make us stronger. We can always decide not to do what another organization does because it does not align with our values, but there is no excuse for failing to gather the information.

Practice humility - Humility is central to being a servant leader and to being effective. It's important to keep our personal identities separate from that of the organizations in which we work. Shared ownership and investment by staff, volunteers, partners, donors, and the Quaker community are critical to the success of any Quaker organization. It's important to be able to receive feedback graciously and then separate what is personal, and what is directed to the position. People can and do angrily disagree with AFSC positions. We are most successful in understanding and incorporating their valid concerns when we can respond with love and respect, even if the answer is, "We see it differently." Leading is about being able to effectively channel the energy and passion of others without absorbing the negative energy or stifling the positive.

Partner - AFSC would have a difficult time achieving any of our goals without partnerships—with the Quaker community, with the communities in which we work, with other Quaker organizations, and with other peace and social justice organizations. Though articulating and conveying a clear sense of identity and purpose is critical to any organization's success, so is the ability to work with others on shared goals, focusing on the desired result and being willing to share credit. Recently AFSC and FCNL worked together to host a joint consultation with many Quaker representatives on "Re-Imagining US Foreign and Security Policy." The effort will result in a joint publication and policy recommendations, along with joint activities to support dialogue within the Quaker world around common principles, as well as larger efforts to gain traction for the ideas put forward.

Regard conflict as creative - Quakers can be more comfortable with the concept than the practice of hearing divergent views as a necessary part of discernment. When people care deeply about an issue or their work, strongly-felt disagreements are inevitable. Explicitly teaching the skills of conflict resolution is an important step to ensure that conflict does not become intractable, but is used creatively to reveal deeper, shared understandings. Quaker-based tools such as Alternatives to Violence Project and Compassionate Listening can be supplemented with secular approaches such as the Harvard Negotiation Project's *Difficult Conversations*. When people in an organization share training in an approach to conflict, it helps establish a context in which expressing divergent opinions is valued and used to expand the wisdom of both the individuals and the group. The ability to 'sit in the fire' and work through these differences with the understanding that greater truth can emerge expands the problem-solving capacity of the organization and all its members.

Place Quaker testimonies at the core – As a Quaker peace and justice organization AFSC needs to be serious about our commitment to the testimonies and to putting the principles of Quaker faith into action. Creating an organization that experiments with living and practicing a Quaker vision of the beloved community becomes challenging when most staff are not members of the Religious Society of Friends. At AFSC we have produced our own introduction to Quaker testimonies to use in orienting staff and volunteers. We believe that it is possible to own our Quaker roots while highlighting the degree to which our principles are reflected in other religions and cultures.

Practicing what we are trying to manifest in the world within the organization is another critical challenge. We need to be in right relationship within our workplaces in order to fulfill our mission beyond our office walls. Different organizations will face different challenges from AFSC's; for example, many Quaker meetings and organizations are sincere in our embrace of the testimony of equality, yet remain overwhelmingly white.

Demonstrate courage and vulnerability - Sometimes the most courageous thing anyone can do is to admit a mistake or acknowledge fallibility. Modeling this for each other and our organizations gives all of us permission to be less than perfect and makes it safer to give each other honest feedback. Being willing to take a stand and stick to it undefensively is also important. Leaders who are unclear about their own commitments make for unclear boundaries and unclear organizational commitments.

"Religion Is A Way of Life"

In a lecture to Harvard divinity students in 1936 Henry Cadbury shared his "personal religion." He began by saying that he was very comfortable leaving open the question of whether God exists or there is life after death. He subscribed to the Quaker tradition that "religion is a way of life," that "the best way to know a religion is to see a religious personality in action." Our Quaker organizations aspire to take this one step further, to let others know our religion by seeing our religious organizations in action. Just as no person can perfectly witness his or her faith, so will our organizations fall short of perfection.

Ultimately, Quaker leadership, like good clerking, requires us as leaders to draw on our best, on that of God in ourselves, to reach out to the best, to that of God in those we seek to lead. We won't always succeed, but when we do, miracles will occur.

ORGANIZATIONAL LEADERSHIP AS A SPIRITUAL GIFT

Doug Bennett

Q UAKERS HAVE a genius for creating organizations that serve a variety of humane purposes. I do not name them all here, but there are enough to give you a sense of the breadth of Friends' contributions to the good of the world.

Earlham College, Guilford College, Haverford College, Swarthmore College, Whittier College, George Fox University, Wilmington College, and several others: All founded by Friends. Has any other religious denomination created a more excellent group of colleges and universities?

Westtown School, Sidwell Friends School, George School, Germantown Friends School, Moses Brown School, Sandy Spring Friends School, Carolina Friends School, Abington Friends School, Olney Friends School, Scattergood Friends School, Friends Seminary, Richmond Friends School, and many, many others: What a terrific array of primary and secondary schools.

Farm and Wilderness Camps, Friends Camp, Friends Music Camp, Camp Dark Waters, Catoctin Quaker Camp, Sierra Friends Camp, Quaker Meadow Christian Camp, and many others: These summer camps have nourished youth for generations.

Friends Fellowship Community, Pennswood Village, Medford Leas,

Stapely in Germantown, Kendal Communities, Foxdale Village, Friends House, Friendsview Retirement Community, Quaker Gardens Senior Living, and many others: Friends' retirement communities have been among the most visionary in terms of caring for the whole person through the aging and dying process.

The Friends Committee on National Legislation and the American Friends Service Committee: Can other religious denominations point to such effective organizations promoting peace and justice in our nation's policies or through direct action and advocacy?

When I say these are wonderful organizations, I mean something like the following. They are institutions that are widely seen (well beyond Friends) as exemplars of excellence. At the same time they are institutions that operate against the grain, refusing to be conformed to this world (Romans 12:2). Typically, Friends' organizations achieve their excellence through building communities characterized by unreserved respect, honesty, and broad participation.

But then we have a counterpoint: the widespread, casual disregard (at times bordering on contempt) with which Friends regard the leadership necessary to these fine organizations. Those who have had leadership responsibility at one of these organizations often quietly express their intense frustration at Friends' attitudes surrounding their work. Their spirits are brought low by the impossible, often nutsy expectations that Friends impose upon their work.

This is quite a paradox, and I am not sure I know how to make sense of it. I would love to understand it, but it is more important that we find a way out of this strange place. The world could use more of our gifts for birthing organizations that serve critical needs. Even more, the world could use our support and sustenance of the organizations we have already created.

Leadership we Quakers may value, but not leadership within organizations. And yet it is within and through organizations that leadership is principally exercised in this world. If we say we reject such organizational leadership, with its necessary deployment of authority and money, then do we not reject organizations? And if so, why have we created so many wonderful organizations? Only to frustrate their functioning?

Growing Into Leadership

I offer myself as one exhibit. I came into adulthood with a deep antipathy toward organizations and organizational leadership. Only slowly did I come to a different view.

Born in 1946, I am at the front edge of the baby boom. Attending Haverford College changed my life and eventually drew me to Quakerism. I graduated in 1968, the year the Vietnam War was at its height, Martin Luther King, Jr. and Bobby Kennedy were assassinated, and urban riots were in the news most weeks. Civil and political rights for African Americans and equality for women were inscribed on the banners of my generation. Before I became a pacifist, before I became a Quaker, I was a member of Students for a Democratic Society.

Growing Up Absurd, the *Port Huron Statement,* and *Reveille for Radicals* shaped my understanding of how I would act in the world. I settled into an oppositional posture. With others in my generation (Trust no one over 30!), I knew what was wrong with the world. We were determined to make it right; task one was to stop the war. From saying no to the Army it was a short step to saying no to corporations and other large organizations.

I came of age, that is, with a decidedly anti-organizational mindset. If I was to do any good in this world, I would do it as a brave individual, working no doubt in solidarity with others. Would I work within the confines of an organization? As little as possible. I went to graduate school, then on to employment in a university as a professor, stridently decrying the cruel idiocies of presidents, provosts, and deans—those in positions of organizational leadership. I consider it one of God's best jokes in my life that I would later become a college provost and then a college president. How did *that* happen?

In graduate school I was fascinated by the inequality of power and what could be done about it. I remember reading E.E. Schattschneider's arresting sentence, "organization is the mobilization of bias." He offered it to explain how some people have much more power than others, even within a democracy where all are equally able to vote. His insight that organizations are the mobilization of bias fit smoothly within my more general critique of organizations as part of the problem.

Then, sometime in my 30s, after I had become a Quaker, I had a slow-

129

firing epiphany. Some organizations could mobilize bias to pursue bad goals, but on the other hand, maybe other organizations could mobilize energy in pursuit of right goals. I began to see the possibility of organizations through which I would want to pour whatever energy or talent I had.

I was invited to become a member of the School Committee at Germantown Friends School. I saw a school, not perfect, but functioning about as well as any human-created school could. I learned a good deal from those in positions of organizational leadership at Germantown Friends. Not long afterward, I was invited to become part of a program committee for the American Friends Service Committee. Again I learned a good deal from watching and talking with those in positions of organizational leadership at AFSC. I learned still more later, as I took on organizational roles, staff and volunteer, at Haverford, Friends Seminary, Earlham and FCNL.

The full form of my epiphany was the realization that I could do very little that was good in the world so long as I saw myself as a pure and determined lone ranger. Instead, what good I might do would largely come by picking well the organizations with which I chose to work, and through those organizations harnessing my energy and talent with others. "Mobilization of bias" took on a more positive cast.

I came to see that organizations vary a great deal in their missions; some had missions I could and should affirm, and others did not. Beyond this, I came to see that some organizations were unusually effective in delivering results given the resources they could deploy, and other organizations were much less effective—even wasteful. I came to think of the better ones as organizations with a high ratio of good outcomes generated to resources used.

I came to think that I should choose to work for organizations whose missions I could strongly affirm and that had those high ratios. Beyond that, I came to think that there was a noble form of work to be had in the care and feeding of such organizations. "Administration" and "management" had been distasteful terms, but over some years I grew more comfortable with them. Most importantly, I learned many of the arts—administrative arts—of nurturing organizations. I have hardly learned them all or learned them well as I should, but I have come to admire and respect those who take on the responsibilities of organizational leadership and perform those duties with diligence and wisdom.

Distrust and Illegitimacy

Wherein lies the frustration felt by those called to leadership in Quaker organizations? In two broad areas, I think. One frustration lies in many Friends' rejection of essential characteristics of organizations. The second frustration arises from an equally deep-seated distrust of organizational leadership among Friends.

A key to understanding both is to recognize that for many Friends, the only legitimate Quaker image of healthy community is a (small) Quaker monthly meeting. Even if we sometimes feel frustrations with them, we treasure our monthly meetings as settings in which we make decisions and take action together. Here we see a right way to do things. By contrast, in other settings—especially large organizations—we see impersonality, corruption and abuse.

Such a monthly meeting numbers its members in the dozens, not the hundreds or thousands. Such a meeting makes all its decisions in a gathering to which all its members have a standing invitation. Actions are not taken until unity is found—unity that is often taken to require the consent of everyone. Relatively little money changes hands. Often there are no paid staff; if there are, the roles of such paid staff (a secretary, a pastor) are circumscribed and carry personal influence rather than positional power. There are few files, manuals or policies. If there are any customers, they are also (at the same time) owners of the enterprise.

Contrast this image of a Quaker meeting as a group of people acting together for common ends within "an organization." Any organization is likely to have greater size, complexity, roles, bureaucracy, fiscal scale and authority relationships. Our image of the Quaker meeting is a standing critique of such organizations with all their worldly trappings.

And yet, Quaker schools, colleges, retirement homes and service organizations all bear the characteristics of organizations more than they resemble Quaker meetings. When they behave like organizations, we are reluctant to claim them as ours—even if we created them.

We imagine, I think, that the organizations we create as Quakers could function like monthly meetings. But they cannot. Even if our schools and colleges are small in relation to non-Quaker schools and colleges, they are still much larger in size than Quaker meetings. That larger scale means larger budgets. It also means our organizations (as opposed to meetings) have greater internal complexity, including differentiated roles. Those differentiated roles imply different bases of expertise, and it makes sense to have those with special expertise make some decisions rather than having everyone participate in every decision. These Quaker organizations serve people who are not members (students, residents, people requiring assistance), and we take on responsibilities to see that we meet their needs effectively and safely. Sensibly, our Quaker organizations do not function like Quaker meetings; but when they do not, we deny them legitimacy.

Those who accept organizational leadership roles within Quaker organizations step straight into that denial. Nearly every action they may take in accord with their responsibilities can be painted as un-Quakerly. What they do (choose one or more) may seem to lack simplicity, or fail to consult everyone sufficiently, or cost too much, or fail to find approval from some people.

Also, think of the phrase "speak truth to power" that comes quickly to our lips when we want to criticize someone in a position of authority. Does it not imply that the powerless have truth and that those with power lack the truth? At some point or other during their service, that bind will weigh down the morale of nearly every leader of every Quaker organization.

Learning to Value Organizational Leadership

Is there a way beyond this? Can we be Quakers and value the organizational leadership that our Quaker organizations need?

In 1 Corinthians 12:4-11, Paul teaches, "(4) there are different kinds of gifts, but the same Spirit distributes them. (5) There are different kinds of service, but the same Lord. (6) There are different kinds of working, but in all of them and in everyone it is the same God at work." In Romans 12: 6-8 (NIV), Paul strikes the same note: "We have different gifts, according to the grace given to each of us."

If your gift is prophesying, then prophesy in accordance with your faith; (7) if it is serving, then serve; if it is teaching, then teach; (8) if it is to encourage, then give encouragement; if it is giving, then give generously; if it is to lead, do it diligently; if it is to show mercy, do it cheerfully.

Is this helpful? Yes, to a degree. Organizational leadership involves some of these, especially (in roughly equal measure) service, encouragement, giving, and leading. It may involve showing mercy occasionally—but rarely if ever can that extend to continuing employment for the incompetent, no matter how a hopelessly ineffective staff member or his friends might urge. Rarely does organizational leadership involve prophesy—optimism, yes, and foresight, too, but rarely prophesy.

But what do service, encouragement, giving, and leading entail? Paul doesn't say much more in Romans. There is virtually nothing about budgets, personnel supervision, policy-making, planning, or outcomes assessment. Should we denigrate these as ungodly gifts—arts to which God calls no one?

What I believe is most important in these two passages is that Paul is quite clear that there are a variety of kinds of spiritual gifts. Goodness doesn't come in just one pattern or flavor, but Paul doesn't mean to give us an exhaustive list.

Quakers today do value a variety of spiritual gifts. We certainly value vocal ministry, service, prophetic witness, and prayer. Can we also value organizational leadership as a spiritual gift? That is the question.

If we insist that the monthly meeting is the only legitimate form of collective endeavor—even subconsciously—then we will not value organizations, and thus we will not be able to value organizational leadership as a spiritual gift. If this is the case, then we should conscientiously refuse to create or to sponsor organizations. We should acknowledge that we were wrong as a Religious Society of Friends to found schools, colleges, camps, retirement communities, and service organizations.

I hope that is not the conclusion we reach. The organizations that Quakers have created do not and cannot function like monthly meetings, "only a little larger." In their operations they should manifest core Quaker testimonies of community simplicity, integrity, equality, and peace. They should be honest, straightforward, and transparent in their dealings. Even if everyone cannot (and should not) participate in the making of every decision, they should take care to listen to everyone, inviting thoughtful contributions from all (students, faculty, residents, etc.) Above all, Quaker organizations should show unreserved respect for all human beings, and they should perform their missions by gathering people into communities where the Divine presence is expected.

By and large this is precisely how Quaker organizations (schools, colleges, camps, retirement homes, service organizations) function today. This is what makes them praiseworthy.

In doing these things, in behaving in these ways, Quaker organizations become witnesses for the Religious Society of Friends. They become our best missions. Many members of Quaker meetings today first encountered Friends at a Friends school or college or camp.

If we are to have Quaker organizations, then we need to embrace them fully and without reservation. That will mean valuing the practices of organizational leadership in the manner of Friends. That will mean valuing the capabilities of personnel supervision, budgeting, timely decision-making, and policy formulation while being straightforward, honest, and respectful to all. We can do this.

CONTRIBUTOR BIOGRAPHIES

Margery Post Abbott has been released by Multnomah Meeting in Portland, Oregon, for a ministry of teaching and writing. Her most recent book, *To Be Broken and Tender*, was published by Western Friend in 2010. Along with co-editing *Walk Worthy of Your Calling: Quakers and the Traveling Ministry* with Peggy Parsons, Marge has two other books about Friends: *A Certain Kind of Perfection* and *The Historical Dictionary of the Friends (Quakers)*, as well as three Pendle Hill pamphlets. She has served as clerk of Multnomah Meeting, North Pacific Yearly Meeting, and of Friends Committee on National Legislation.

Neal Andrews is a Councilman in the city of Ventura, California. He serves on the Board of Directors of the California League of Cities and has chaired the National League of Cities prestigious National Policy Committee on Community & Economic Development. His career has included time as a university professor, an executive in one of the largest health care organizations in the country, a business owner, and in management at multiple levels of government. He has also served on many boards of directors of charitable or professional organizations. He is affiliated with the Santa Barbara Friends Meeting.

Doug Bennett served as President of Earlham College from 1997 to 2011. Previously he held positions as a faculty member or administrator at the American Council of Learned Societies, Reed College, and Temple University. Within the world of Friends he has served on governing boards and committees for Haverford College, Friends Seminary (NYC), Germantown Friends School, the Friends Association for Higher Education, the Friends Committee on National Legislation, and the American Friends Service Committee. A convinced Quaker, he belongs to First Friends Meeting in Richmond, Indiana. He now lives in Maine, and blogs about religious matters on riverviewfriend.wordpress.com.

Christine Betz Hall is a member of Whidbey Island Friends Meeting, which upholds her ministry through an anchor committee. As an experienced educator, spiritual director, and retreat leader, she is called to nurture faithfulness and strengthen contemporary expressions of Spirit-led ministry within and beyond The Religious Society of Friends. She teaches in the ecumenical school of Theology and Ministry at Seattle University, and directs a retreat-study program for unprogrammed and Evangelical Quakers in the Northwest U.S.—Way of the Spirit: Contemplative Study in Community. Her non-profit home base for discernment, board accountability and fundraising is Good News Associates: http://goodnewsassoc.org.

Shan Cretin is the General Secretary of the American Friends Service Committee. Prior to her appointment in 2010, she served as Director of the AFSC's Pacific Southwest Region for seven years, responsible for programs in Southern California, Hawaii, Arizona, and New Mexico. She has served as Clerk of Pacific Yearly Meeting, co-founded the Los Angeles chapter of Alternatives to Violence Project, and serves on the board of directors of The California Endowment. She is a graduate of and has taught at the Massachusetts Institute of Technology and Yale University and has also taught at Harvard University, West China Medical University, Shanghai Medical University, and the University of California at Los Angeles.

C. Wess Daniels is a released minister at Camas Friends Church, a PhD student in the School of Intercultural Studies at Fuller Theological Seminary, and an adjunct professor at George Fox Seminary. Equally important in his life are his three young children and his wife, Emily. Wess enjoys roasting coffee, reading and writing, spending time outdoors and playing imaginative games with his kids. Find him at gatheringinlight.com.

Eleanor Dart spent many months over a five-year period working as a civilian counselor on U.S. Military bases during the wars in Iraq and Afghanistan. She is a life-time Quaker and a member of Pima Monthly Meeting in Tucson, Arizona.

Bill and Genie Durland are members of Colorado Springs Meeting, and live in Cokedale, Colorado. For more than forty years, Bill has practiced law, with an emphasis on human rights and civil liberties. He is also an educator and the author of several books, with a new title coming out in 2013. Bill served in the Virginia House of Delegates, and has held other elected positions. Both he and Genie are devoted activists for peace and social justice in Palestine.

Lucy Duncan is AFSC's Friends Liaison. She has been a storyteller for almost twenty years and in the past five years has begun working with Quaker meetings to help Friends to tell their stories of spiritual experience. Before coming to AFSC, Lucy worked as the bookstore manager, then Director of Communications at Friends General Conference. Lucy is a member of Goshen Friends Meeting of Philadelphia Yearly Meeting. She lives at Friends Southwestern Burial Ground in the caretaker's house with her husband, Graham, and their 11-year-old son, Simon. She writes and edits the AFSC blog Acting in Faith at www.afsc.org/friends.

Dorsey Green lives in Seattle, Washington and is a member of University Meeting of North Pacific Yearly Meeting. She has been privileged to clerk the Friends Committee on National Legislation as well as her monthly and yearly meetings. She is a psychologist in independent practice and an adjunct clinical instructor at the University of Washington. Dorsey lives with her partner Ann, and has two sons, two grandsons, a daughter-in-law, an extended family which includes Ann's children and grandchildren, and a lovely, old Norwegian Elkhound.

Nadine Hoover is a member of Alfred Friends Meeting (NY), coordinates Friends Peace Teams in Asia West Pacific, directs Conscience Studio, facilitates Alternatives to Violence Project workshops, teaches karate and body-mind centering and offers massage therapy. She is a graduate of George School and Friends World College. With a doctorate from Florida State University, she worked on international education grants in Indonesia for two decades and founded numerous developmental schools. She served as Southeastern Yearly Meeting's Secretary, Friends General Conference's bookstore manager and carries with her a travel minute from New York Yearly Meeting.

Nancy Irving is a member of Olympia (WA) Friends Meeting. She is a graduate of George School, the University of Pennsylvania, and Lewis & Clark Law School. Prior to serving as General Secretary of Friends World Committee for Consultation, based in the World Office in London, she worked as an attorney and business trade association executive in Washington State, Oregon, and Pennsylvania. Following her work in London, she was the Cadbury Scholar at Pendle Hill Quaker Study Center. Nancy's experience includes service on numerous Quaker committees and boards as well as service with secular organizations. She was one of the organizers of the first Northwest Women's Theological Conference.

Laura Magnani is Interim Regional Director for the American Friends Service Committee, Pacific Mountain Region. Most of her work has been in the area of criminal justice. From 1971-1979 she was the lobbyist for the Friends Committee on Legislation in Sacramento, California. She is author of *America's First Penitentiary: A Two Hundred Year Old Failure* (2000), and co-author with the late Harmon Wray of *Beyond Prisons: A New Interfaith Paradigm for Our Failed Prison System* (2006, Augsburg/Fortress Press). She is also adjunct faculty at Starr King School for the Ministry, teaching classes in prisons and restorative justice. Laura has also been involved in the peace movement throughout her adult life, seeing work to end violence around the world as central to her faith life. She is a member of Strawberry Creek Meeting in Berkeley, CA.

Stephen McNeil, San Francisco, California, is the Wage Peace Director with American Friends Service Committee, U.S. West Region in San Francisco. He has served as an intern (1976), clerk of Policy, Development, Executive and General Committees of FCNL. He is currently on the board of Volunteers in Asia which supports young adult exchanges and placements in Asia. Since 2004 he has served with the San Francisco Bay Area Darfur Coalition, an anti-genocide group made up of survivors and descendants of past and current genocides. He is a member of Strawberry Creek Monthly Meeting in Berkeley.

Robin Mohr serves as Executive Secretary for the Section of the Americas of the Friends World Committee for Consultation. She is also a writer, minister and mother. Her blog, *What Canst Thou Say?* can be found at robinmsf.blogspot.com. She coined the term "convergent Friends" in late 2005 to describe a movement of the Holy Spirit among Friends across divides of age, geography and theology. She recently transferred her membership to Green Street Monthly Meeting in Philadelphia Yearly Meeting from San Francisco Monthly Meeting in Pacific Yearly Meeting.

Peggy Senger Parsons is a recorded Friends minister and licensed professional counselor who lives in Salem, Oregon. Peggy was the founding pastor of Freedom Friends Church, a Christ-centered, inclusive, pastoral Quaker meeting. A major focus of hers for the last decade has been trauma healing, especially among Quakers in Central Africa. Peggy is a four-time author and host of the blog sillypoorgospel. blogspot.com. She is presently ministering in higher education.

Diane Randall joined Friends Committee on National Legislation in

2011 as the fourth Executive Secretary since 1943. Her background includes many years as an executive director of statewide advocacy organizations, a passion for rebuilding the democratic system in our country, a record of achievements in lobbying and citizen engagement and a spiritual grounding in the Religious Society of Friends. An active member of Hartford Monthly Meeting (CT), New England Yearly Meeting, Diane has served as clerk of her monthly meeting and clerk of most committees in the meeting as well serving on the Development, Worship and Counsel, and Nominating Committees of New England Yearly Meeting; and on the Board of Advisors of the Earlham School of Religion.

Ann Stever became a member of University Meeting (Seattle) in 1965. She has held volunteer and staff leadership positions in the American Friends Service Committee, as a National Board member, clerk of the Regional Executive Committee twice and as Regional Executive Secretary. Ann has clerked both University Meeting and North Pacific Yearly Meeting, and currently serves on the Executive Committee of Friends World Committee for Consultation Section of the Americas. She and Dorsey Green were married under the care of University Meeting in 1998, and it is a delight to her that her three adult children and five grandchildren all live near Seattle.

Nancy Thomas identifies herself first of all as a disciple of Jesus. She is wife to her best friend, Hal, and mother and grandmother to some beautiful people. As a member of North Valley Friends Church in Northwest Yearly Meeting, she enjoys participating in both unprogrammed and programmed worship. Nancy has worked all her life in Latin America, among Quakers, and presently, with a leadership development program known as PRODOLA. She is also a writer and a lover of language, and blogs at www.nancyjthomas.blogspot.com.

Joe Volk retired as Executive Secretary of Friends Committee on National Legislation (FCNL) in February 2011. Among his activities in more than 30 years working for peace, social justice, and environmental balance, Joe has lobbied Congress to support peaceful prevention of deadly conflict, nuclear disarmament, peace in Iraq, and many other issues. Prior to joining FCNL in 1990, Joe worked 18 years for the American Friends Service Committee (AFSC) and served as its National Secretary for Peace Education from 1982 to 1990. He was the first Friend in Residence at Haverford College and serves on the Wilmington College Board of Trustees, and the board of The Kendal Corporation.

Ashley M. Wilcox is a member of Freedom Friends Church in Salem, Oregon and a graduate of the School of the Spirit Ministry's program "On Being a Spiritual Nurturer," class of 2011. She served as clerk of Freedom Friends in 2011-12 and was co-clerk of the planning committee for the 2010 Pacific Northwest Quaker Women's Theology Conference. Ashley has traveled in the ministry as a minister and an elder and carries a concern for supporting ministers in the Religious Society of Friends. Her writing has been published in *Western Friend*, *Friends Journal*, various Quaker anthologies, and on her blog, www.questforadequacy.blogspot.com.

ADDITIONAL RESOURCES
FOR DEVELOPING LEADERSHIP IN THE MANNER OF FRIENDS

This is not an exhaustive list of resources and opportunities, but it is a place to begin exploring, should you wish to deepen your understanding of Quakers and leadership.

Educational Programs and Events

Earlham School of Religion, a Christian graduate theological school in the Quaker tradition, offers a **Leadership Studies** track in its graduate program. They also host an annual **Leadership Conference** in the summer that is open to everyone; videos and proceedings of past conferences are available on the ESR website. ESR is located in Richmond, Indiana; find them online at http://esr.earlham.edu/.

George Fox University in Newberg, Oregon, has a **Friends Leadership** Program for undergraduates. The program website is http://www.georgefox.edu/friends-leadership/index.html.

The **Good News Associates,** a Quaker-run nonprofit Christian organization supporting individuals in ministry, runs an annual **Leadership Institute for Group Discernment**. Held at Tillikum Retreat Center in Newberg, Oregon, the three-day program is an intensive training in Friends' practices, geared toward church leadership of any denomination.

Guilford College in Greensboro, North Carolina, has an intensive, faculty-supported program for students called the **Quaker Leadership Scholars Program**. Approximately fifty students commit to engage in service and to learn about Quaker practices and principles. More information is at http://www.guilford.edu/about-guilford/quaker-heritage/quaker-leadership-scholars-program/.

Each summer, **Pendle Hill** Quaker retreat center in Waillingford, Pennsylvania, organizes a **Young Adult Friends Conference** (formerly known as the Young Adult Leadership Development Program) to bring together Quakers age 18-35 from around the country to explore the skills and spiritual development required to be effective change agents in the world. Learn more at http://www.pendlehill.org/yald.

Books and Pamphlets

Leading Quakers: Discipleship Leadership, A Friends Model
by Jennie Isbel
This is a practical guide for a year-long adult religious education program, designed to develop and foster Quaker-style leadership in congregations.

Lives That Speak: Stories of Twentieth-Century Quakers
edited by Marnie Clark
Designed for 4th-8th graders, this collection of short biographies of contemporary Quaker leaders is insightful for older Friends, too. Questions and activities accompany each chapter.

Practicing Discernment Together:
Finding God's Way Forward In Decision Making
by Lon Fendall, Jan Wood, and Bruce Bishop
A deep and thorough exploration of how Friends listen as a group for the will of the Divine, written by three gifted leaders from the evangelical Quaker tradition.

Servant Leadership:
A Journey into the Nature of Legitimate Power and Greatness
by Robert Greenleaf
Greenleaf's classic collection of essays coined the term "servant leadership" over twenty-five years ago, and today it continues to inspire Friends and those in leadership positions the world over.

Soul At Work:
Spiritual Leadership In Organizations
by Margaret Benefiel
A Quaker's take on finding soul in the workplace, explored through profiles of well-known businesses and individuals.

Beyond Consensus:
Salvaging the Sense of the Meeting
by Barry Morley
This Pendle Hill pamplet presents a beautiful and personal exploration of the relationship between worship and the sense of the meeting. This should be required reading for every Friend.
Leadership And Authority In The Religious Society Of Friends
by Arthur Larrabee
The General Secretary of Philadelphia Yearly Meeting, one of the larger Quaker organizations in the US, reflects on the contemporary Quaker's fear of leadership in this short pamphlet.

Powerful Beyond Measure:
the Legacy of Quaker Leadership in the 21st Century
by George Lakey
In this pamphlet, lifelong activist and social change consultant George Lakey addresses the need to confront issues of class prejudice as we strive to develop leadership for social change.

Tall Poppies:
Supporting Gifts of Ministry and Eldering in Monthly Meetings
by Martha Paxson Grundy
Grundy offers a careful and accessible account of the traditional Quaker understanding of power and spiritual authority in this pamphlet.

All books and pamphlets are available through http://www.quakerbooks.org.

Enlivened by the Mystery: Quakers and God
#1 in the Giving Form to Faith series

edited by Kathy Hyzy

This is the first book in the Giving Form to Faith series, which explores the ways in which Quakers express their faith, their Quakerness, in the world.

How have you experienced God or the Divine?

With this query, Western Friend invited Quakers across the West to share their stories through art, poetry, fiction and essays. The contributions of over fifty Friends are gathered in this testament to the breadth of spiritual experience in the Religious Society of Friends.

Contributors include: Marge Abbott, Heidi Blocher, Eleanor Dart, Iris Graville, Robert Griswold, Susan Merrill, Markley Morris, Rob Pierson, Trudy Reagan, Eric Sabelman, Biliana Stremska, Lynn Waddington, Nancy Wood, and many others.

To Be Broken and Tender:
A Quaker Theology for Today

by Margery Post Abbott

In *To Be Broken and Tender*, Friend and Quaker historian Margery Abbott weaves together a brave and beautiful personal narrative with Quaker history and theological reflection in response to questions and struggles about belief, language, social issues and other deeply-felt concerns that unsettle and divide our meetings and the wider Religious Society of Friends. A study guide assists readers in their own discernment around challenging issues such as care for the environment, our personal relationships to God and Christianity, and the role Friends have in making the world right.

Compassionate Listening
and Other Writings by Gene Knudsen Hoffman

edited by Anthony Manousos

NEW foreword by Leah Green,
founder of The Compassionate Listening Project

Quaker Gene Knudsen Hoffman dedicated much of her life to seeking out the deep, psychological causes of violence and to helping bring about healing and reconciliation through a process she calls "Compassionate Listening." Her work inspired Leah Green to begin The Compassionate Listening Project, whose workshops have taught hundreds of people how to listen with their hearts as well as minds. This collection of writings sheds light on Hoffman's life and inspiration.

EarthLight: Spiritual Wisdom for an Ecological Age

edited by Cindy Spring and Anthony Manousos

During its fifteen years of publication, *EarthLight* magazine celebrated the living Earth and our thirteen billion year story of the universe. Founded and inspired by Quakers, *EarthLight* featured articles by the world's seminal figures in secular and religious thought about the place and participation of humankind in creation. This anthology embodies the best of *EarthLight* and of Quaker writers on spirituality and ecology during the past twenty years. Contributors include Maya Angelou, Thomas Berry, Jim Corbett, Joanna Macy, Terry Tempest Williams and many others.

CPSIA information can be obtained at www.ICGtesting.com
Printed in the USA
BVOW04s1557190913

331496BV00002B/74/P